"Debra Cohen provides a powerful, practical framework that can help any manager to reach their true potential!" – **Marc Effron, President, The Talent Strategy Group, USA**

"This self-help book proves there is always something new to learn. It clearly explains concepts, gives practical examples, and challenges you to organize and record your approach to your own learning. Whatever stage you are at in your management career it inspires you to try something new and do what you do better. A book worth keeping to hand when you need to energize your next steps and those of others around you." – **Caroline Brent, Senior Vice President, Future Talent Council, Stockholm, Sweden**

"*Developing Management Proficiency* is a book that will challenge managers to take charge of developing their everyday management skills using self-directed learning tools. Dr. Cohen provides practical tools and examples that are on point for all managers – including those who don't yet manage people." – **Gary Latham, Secretary of State Professor of Organizational Effectiveness, Rotman School of Management, University of Toronto**

Developing Management Proficiency

Developing Management Proficiency: A Self-Directed Learning Approach is a pragmatic, easy-to-follow roadmap for managers to help develop the behaviors and skills necessary for success.

Strong behavioral competencies are essential for any manager today. Emphasizing a self-directed learning approach, this book is designed to transform passive learners into active learners by helping to develop behavioral skills, based on individual needs. By providing the reader with the tools for self-directed learning, Deb Cohen provides an unending mechanism to learn, improve, and grow, helping develop the proficiencies needed to be successful in doing their job or advancing in their career. With features such as practical examples, worksheets, tables, and figures, the book is packed full of self-directed learning activities including role play, observation, networking, journaling, and questioning, all powerful drivers of learning and development.

With expert guidance on how to approach personal development in day-to-day activities rather than in a formal course setting, this book is an essential resource for managers at all levels, as well as anyone training or interested in a managerial role.

Deb Cohen, Ph.D., is a management and HR expert. She is a writer, speaker, trainer, and consultant. Deb has 30 years' experience as an association executive and business school professor.

Developing Management Proficiency

A Self-Directed Learning Approach

Deb Cohen

Routledge
Taylor & Francis Group

NEW YORK AND LONDON

First published 2020
by Routledge
52 Vanderbilt Avenue, New York, NY 10017

and by Routledge
2 Park Square, Milton Park, Abingdon, Oxon, OX14 4RN

Routledge is an imprint of the Taylor & Francis Group, an informa business

© 2020 Taylor & Francis

Library of Congress Cataloging-in-Publication Data
A catalog record for this title has been requested

ISBN: 978-0-367-25307-3 (hbk)
ISBN: 978-0-367-25310-3 (pbk)
ISBN: 978-0-429-28711-4 (ebk)

Typeset in Bembo
by Newgen Publishing UK

Visit the eResources: www.routledge.com/9780367253103

This book is dedicated to my son, Jacob, because he is the light of my life and motivates me to be the best that I can be and to be a role model that I hope he appreciates. And this book is also dedicated to my mom, Sandy, who is not here to see this publication but who was always proud of me.

Contents

List of Figures, Tables, Worksheets, and Examples

1 Introduction

In today's fast-paced business environment, where staying competitive and being recognized for your leadership and management proficiency is critical, many of us need to turn inward for motivation and direction in building behaviors for success. Behavioral competencies are essential for success for any manager today. This book is a roadmap for managers to help you develop the behaviors necessary to be successful. You will find this to be a pragmatic and easy-to-follow book that is supplemented with practical exercises, worksheets, tables, and figures that will be useful to managers whether you are an individual contributor or a people manager. It will be useful to leaders who manage managers and anyone who aspires to be a leader or manager. The book is designed to transform passive learners into active learners by helping managers develop behavioral and other competencies at their own pace and based on individual needs. Included is guidance on how to approach personal development in day-to-day activities rather than only in a formal course setting. Self-directed learning activities such as role play, observation, and networking can be powerful drivers of learning and development and allow the learners to be autonomous and in charge of their future.

This book focuses on helping you develop the proficiencies needed to be successful in doing a job or advancing in your career, and it emphasizes a self-directed learning approach to accomplish development. There are many ways, both formal and informal, of developing the skills and abilities needed to do your job and to advance in your career. Self-directed learning is an approach where the individual takes the initiative and responsibility to learn what they need in the short-term *and* long-term to be successful and then execute a learning plan.

Why become a self-directed learner?

- You know yourself better than anyone.
- Adults learn best through experience.
- Organizations may not provide all the learning opportunities needed.
- Your development is your responsibility.

As you read this book, you will find a plan of action for any manager at any level of experience, to build a customized development plan to evolve competencies for higher job and career success. The underlying construct in the book is similar in concept to *"Give a man a fish, and he will eat for a day. Teach a man how to fish, and you feed him for a lifetime."*[1] In other words, the approach emphasizes that it is more beneficial to learn the nuances of self-directed learning, than it is to list the competencies needed, describe them, and suggest ways you can develop them. Give a manager the tools for self-directed learning, and you give them an unending mechanism to learn, improve, and grow. Self-directed learning is an approach that can be used over time to hone your proficiency and build on what is needed by incorporating the plan into everyday activities. It is inherently customizable to your needs.

Books and articles abound about how to be a better manager and the competencies needed to advance your career. These texts tend to focus on specific managerial or leadership skillsets. They describe the competencies and may make suggestions as to *how* to develop these managerial proficiencies. Taking an approach that emphasizes self-directed learning as a process to apply to build any management competency that may be needed, now or in the future, sets a manager up for success through *their* efforts regardless of the organization in which they work. Rather than only describing the self-directed learning activity, Chapters 5 through 9 provide worksheets, figures, tables, and examples that highlight important managerial behaviors. The book suggests relevant competencies, and learning tools, offering 50 competencies that are critical to all organizations. The 50 competencies are described and used throughout the book as illustrations, but the list itself is not meant to be exhaustive.

Part One: Setting the Stage

Learning and the resulting behavior change for adult professionals best occurs through experience and reflection. Experiential activities place people directly within a particular situation and allow them to apply what they are learning more effectively. Managers need to be active partners in learning new concepts and in developing and strengthening behaviors. Activities that engage individuals in actual, ongoing work can serve as a powerful mechanism for behavior change. Experience in and of itself may not be the sole mechanism for learning, but a reflection on the experience can yield wisdom and insight that will be invaluable for effective development of your knowledge, skills, abilities, and other characteristics (KSAOs). The first section of the book, Chapters 2 through 4, set the stage for the self-directed learning tools described in the second section.

Management Competencies

Management competencies are the skills, attitudes, and abilities necessary to do a job. Research has shown that some of the competencies commonly used across disciplines by successful managers include: communication skills, team-working, self-management, strategic-orientation, decision making, risk-taking, and creativity.[2] It is easier to measure hard skills like financial expertise yet more challenging to measure less-tangible skills like effective communication or teamwork. To advance our performance as employees and coworkers, we must learn which competencies are necessary for our role and account for the fact that our roles regularly change, as does what is expected of us. What is needed today may not be sufficient for success tomorrow. Chapter 2 focuses on the importance of aligning competencies with a person's role today and anticipating future needs. A time and need orientation framework is presented, as is a description of 50 essential competencies. The concept of proficiency levels is discussed, and three managers are introduced as case examples, which will form the basis for illustrations throughout the book.

Self-directed Learning

Self-directed learning is a process in which people take the initiative, with or without the help of others, to identify their learning needs, formulate personal learning goals, identify the resources for active learning, then select and apply appropriate mechanisms to facilitate learning. This means that the individual is taking responsibility for all aspects of learning and development. Self-directed learning does not mean that learning activities are done solely by yourself, nor does it mean that all activities are decided on and executed without assistance. The learner typically owns the final decision of who is involved. Self-directed learners generally are motivated, tend to be persistent, are independent, are usually self-disciplined, set their goals and remain goal oriented, and develop more self-confidence over time. Chapter 3 discusses self-directed learning as a professional development tool for managers. The chapter describes how adult learners are different, compares self-directed learning to face-to-face learning, and provides a six-step process for self-directed learning. A comparative hierarchy for self-directed learning depicting both the employee and employer perspectives is presented, as is a self-directed learning continuum.

Self-assessment

Self-assessment, to be effective, should consider an individual's work-related values, interests, personality type, and aptitudes.[3] These personal characteristics make up who you are, and are typically considered when thinking about what to study in school or what career to pursue. Another context in which self-assessment is essential is when a performance evaluation system requires input from the individual, not just your supervisor. Several factors need to be considered, and ignoring the facts about who you are won't give you an accurate picture. In the context of this book and specifically in the context of this chapter, the discussion includes how to evaluate the competencies you need now and those to anticipate as your role and career evolve. Chapter 4 focuses on how to do an initial self-assessment and then how to regularly update the self-assessment by providing worksheets to help you assess your proficiency level, and emphasizes how important the competencies are to you and your future. Suggestions for establishing a professional development plan are presented. Distinctions between formal and informal assessments are made, as are suggestions for how to regularly update your self-assessment.

Part Two: Self-directed Learning Activities

Section Two concentrates on self-directed learning activities. Each of the five chapters describes a unique method, how to use it, and when the application may be most effective. Each chapter presents comparisons, examples, tools, exercises, worksheets, suggestions, and figures to make the content practical and useful. Figure 1.1 shows the five mechanisms for self-directed learning that are discussed in this section. These learning methods are both independent and supportive of one another and each represents a spoke in the wheel of self-directed learning. Each of these approaches can be described from a research perspective, but the plan for the book is to address each as an "art." The "art" of something typically refers to a skill that is developed through study, experience, or observation. Some examples of well-known things referred to as "art" are the *Art of War*, a book about strategy, by Sun Tzu,[4] the *Art of Gathering*,[5] about how we interact in groups, or the *Art of Seduction*,[6] a book about social power. The meat of this book explores five "arts" for self-directed learning that, when taken together, represent a way for managers to acquire, and continually evolve, the proficiency they need to be competent throughout their managerial life. Each chapter concludes with detailed tips on how to use the tool and how to use it more effectively.

The Art of Networking

Networking is both an art and a science. It has the overall purpose of building professional relationships. Networking, at its core, is an exchange between two people and typically involves the cultivation of long-term and productive relationships. Because networking is a process that nurtures the exchange of information and ideas among individuals, it can facilitate learning and development. Although networking is a ubiquitous tool and it is often informal. Those who engage in networking rarely prepare with structure and forethought. Chapter 5 discusses how

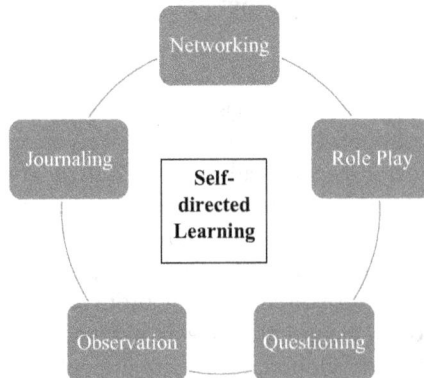

Figure 1.1 The Art of Self-directed Learning for Developing Management Proficiency

to approach networking with a definitive purpose to develop self-identified needs for prioritized competencies. Building and cultivating professional relationships can influence the quality of your work and have a positive impact on your performance. The chapter discusses the differences between networking inside and outside an organization as well as with family and friends. Sources for networking are identified, and traditional networking is compared to a self-directed learning perspective of networking.

The Art of Role Playing

Role play can be a powerful tool to help develop effective behavior as a manager. While role playing can hone your demeanor to be both more comfortable and more effective, role playing need not be a burden to use or develop. Role play can be employed almost daily as a tool to practice and build skills. It is easy to do by yourself, with one other person, or with multiple people. Once a comfort level with doing role play is developed, it becomes like a pen or a wallet that you easily carry with you and can draw on to use when the time is right. There are myriad opportunities for using and applying role play to your development in natural ways. Chapter 6 presents suggestions for how to use role playing as an individual activity or one with a partner. The chapter describes when and how to use role play, the benefits of role playing as well as the drawbacks or when to limit this approach. In addition to examples, many role play scenarios to be used for practice are provided.

The Art of Questioning

The Socratic method is often thought of as a form of teaching or as a teaching tactic. It can be a powerful method for directing a learner toward critical thinking. The leader of the dialogue in the Socratic method asks probing questions with the objective of developing critical thought – typically in the area of values, beliefs, and principles. This method has shown that asking questions can lead to a greater understanding of a person's actions in a given context and of which behaviors may be more effective than others. If we are to learn from others' reactions and behaviors and develop our behaviors and actions, we need to know how to gather, process, and filter the information. One way to do this is by asking better questions and by being systematic in how we approach asking questions and engaging in discussions. Chapter 7 focuses on how to build and participate in a questioning strategy. Question types are defined, and illustrations for each type of question are applied to management competencies. A plan for question development is offered, and examples are included.

The Art of Observation

Observation involves careful watching or listening. The art of observation can be formal or informal and is driven by your own volition. Observation consists of taking note of specific facts or behaviors and recognizing patterns – or the lack of patterns. It may include making a mental note of something or taking notes. Observational learning describes the process of learning by watching or observing others, retaining the information, and then later replicating the behaviors that were seen. Observation is usually combined with other learning tools such as networking, journaling, and day-to-day interactions. Chapter 8 provides a roadmap of how to approach observation systematically and effectively to develop your managerial behavior. The science behind observation, social learning theory, is discussed in a practical way followed by the who, what, where, why, and when components of observation. An approach to developing an observation schedule is offered.

The Art of Journaling

Journaling is a way to record your insights and ideas, and it is a way to solidify your concerns and insights. It is also a way to learn about your competencies – with an eye toward improving them. A journal is where you begin identifying how others demonstrate their skill and where you start to think about how you might change your behavioral competencies. It is also where you can strategize and plan the execution of developing effective behaviors in a variety of contexts. A journal provides a framework for making ideas into something much more tangible. Chapter 9 compares why some people gravitate toward keeping a journal, and others do not. The chapter focuses on why journaling can be beneficial and provides detail on how to create and sustain a journal for learning. The chapter is also designed to help those who have never journaled to gain a comfort level in doing so.

Part Three: Conclusion and an Illustration

After setting the stage in Section One and detailing the five tools for self-directed learning in Section Two, Section Three pulls all the information together and provides suggestions and more tools for putting everything into practice, highlighting the value of a self-directed mindset. An appendix with an integrative case illustration is provided.

The Path Forward

Chapter 10 focuses on the need to incorporate self-direction into everyday practice and to maintain a focus to keep up with learning continuously. The aim of *Developing Management Proficiency* is to inspire the reader and any manager or aspiring manager to reflect on what competencies you need to be successful and to seek to develop these competencies. Management is a process, and the capacity to grow as a manager will ultimately determine your future success. This chapter expands the view of self-directed learning and includes worksheets and illustrations of how to capture learning moments and how to deal with new or immediate challenges that may not have been uncovered during a self-assessment. Embracing lifelong learning using a self-directed approach provides lasting benefits and can be applied to all your learning needs – not just the ones you may prioritize in a self-assessment.

Appendix: Case Illustration

The case of Ben, a manager who has been offered an opportunity to take on a career-changing assignment, is presented. This case shows how one individual can apply self-directed learning to make a career decision, and build a plan for self-directed learning to be more effective in a new opportunity.

Notes

1 This saying is usually attributed to Confucius.
2 https://apps2.campusservices.harvard.edu/cas/empldocs/cs/harvard_competency_ dictionary_complete.pdf; https://core.ac.uk/download/pdf/82542094.pdf – Bucur, I. (2013). Managerial Core Competencies as Predictors of Managerial Performance, on Different Levels of Management. *Procedia – Social and Behavioral Sciences*, 78, 365–369.
3 https://blog.clearcompany.com/self-assessment-examples-prove-your-worth
4 https://jamesclear.com/book-summaries/the-art-of-war
5 www.priyaparker.com/
6 www.nateliason.com/notes/art-seduction-robert-greene

Bibliography

Bucur, I. (2013). Managerial Core Competencies as Predictors of Managerial Performance, on Different Levels of Management. *Procedia – Social and Behavioral Sciences*, Vol. 78, 365–369.
Greene, R. (2004). *The Art of Seduction*. London: Profile Books.
Harvard University (retrieved July, 2019). Competency Dictionary. Available: https:// apps2.campusservices.harvard.edu/cas/empldocs/cs/harvard_competency_dictionary_ complete.pdf
Parker, P. (2018). *The Art of Gathering*. New York: Penguin Random House.
Pollack, S. (retrieved July, 2019). 9 Self-assessment Examples to Prove Your Worth. Available: https://blog.clearcompany.com/self-assessment-examples-prove-your-worth
Tzu, S. (1996). *The Art of War*. North Clarendon: Tuttle Publishing.

Part I

2 Management Competencies

Managers are those responsible for controlling people and programs in organizations. As a person "in charge" of something, a manager must be able to handle many things; including supervising people and overseeing activities. What managerial competencies does it take to be successful and to thrive as a manager or as your job and role evolves? Do competencies that you develop during one part of your education and career stay with you? Do they change over time? How do you know if you have the competencies you need? How do you know if you have the right level of expertise? Have you considered what you may need now compared to the future? How often should you do a self-assessment and when should you ask others for feedback? Also, how do you ensure that your competencies are aligned with your role and your aspirations? All of these are important questions and ones that managers concerned about developing their skills should be asking. This chapter focuses on defining important competencies and discussing the need to align competency needs today and in the future, as well as understanding your proficiency levels for how you perform.

Management Effectiveness

Managerial competencies are the skills, attitudes, and abilities necessary to do a job. Research has shown that some of the competencies commonly used across disciplines by successful managers include: communication skills, team-working, self-management, result-orientation, strategic-orientation, decision making, risk-taking, and creativity.[1] On top of these behavioral competencies, requirements such as financial acumen and technical skills also exist. It may be far easier to measure hard skills like financial expertise yet far more challenging to measure less-tangible skills like effective teamwork, motivation, and other behavioral assets a manager may possess. Behavioral competencies, while more difficult to evaluate or measure, are often more critical for success. Managerial competencies play an important role today and are often relegated, concerning development, to a back-seat position by organizations and managers themselves. To move the performance of employees, coworkers, and ourselves further, we must learn which skills are necessary for our role and account for the fact that our roles change regularly, as does what is expected of us.

When a manager is deemed competent, it may be tempting to assume that he or she has attained proficiency in a set of static skills or attributes related to success in their field or for a particular role. The reality is that the behaviors associated with these skills and attributes are far from static. Furthermore, the technical expertise that got you noticed and moved you into a managerial role may not be sufficient for success in a managerial position or future roles. Also, managerial competence should not be confused with performance in a role, since performance, as we know, can be variable regardless of the level of proficiency one reaches for any given competency. Perhaps more critical is the fact that strong skills and behaviors associated with one competency or a group of competencies does not ensure strong behavior or skill in all competencies.

Competencies are identified through the study of jobs themselves. A list, of competencies, can provide a nice view of the range of possible competencies; however, to determine what a person needs to be able to do in a job, the job itself must be studied and analyzed. A job analysis provides valuable insight that helps organizations know the qualifications to seek as well as things like how to price the job in the context of the organization and the job market as a whole. Technical competencies can more easily be tested by organizations to determine if the skill and knowledge necessary for success are present – but it is the behavioral competencies that, in combination with technical expertise, will more likely predict and ensure success. Some competencies are both technical and behavioral.

Technical Versus Behavioral Competencies

Behavioral competencies are distinct from technical competencies. Technical competencies are typically learned in a more formal education or training setting and often on the job. They include skills like writing, budgeting, marketing, engineering, math, and compliance. Behavioral competencies, on the other hand, are learned both formally and informally through training, education, and primarily through experience. They include skills like decisiveness, integrity, dealing with pressure, relationship management, and many more. As people progress through their career or ascend in an organization, their behavioral competencies often determine, to a greater extent, their selection and success as managers and leaders. Moreover, different positions require different types and ranges of behavioral competencies for success. Most importantly, as the business environment changes, managers in an organization may need different behavioral competencies to be effective in new situations.

One easy way to distinguish between technical and behavioral competencies is that technical competencies are what a person can do, whereas behavioral competencies demonstrate how a person performs in their role. Technical competencies tend to define specific knowledge or hard skills that an individual possesses, whereas behavioral competencies are broader, often explaining what a person does or should do as they perform their role. For example, a worker in the hospitality industry would need technical expertise concerning customer service and quality assurance; and at an industry level, they may need hotel management experience and an understanding of relevant laws and regulations. On the behavioral side, skills such as listening, initiative, and problem-solving may be essential. An IT professional may need empathy, attention to detail, and teamwork concerning behavioral competencies and will require knowledge of operating systems, integration, and security protocols on the technical side. There may be organization-specific and occupation-specific protocols that must be followed.

Although technical and behavioral competencies may have different roots and implications for individuals and their roles, you will seldom find one without the other. Sometimes within a single competency, you need to be able to identify both the technical and behavioral parts to be effective as well as recognize how competencies overlap and complement one another. For example, negotiation is a skill that involves specific steps and tactics; however, someone negotiating must know industry trends as well as possess the ability to read emotions and nonverbal cues to be successful in working toward an amicable resolution. While there may be many different competencies needed, and that you possess, your expertise, skill, and ability on each is what will distinguish you as highly qualified.

Competency Models

Competency models have been available for the past four or five decades but have come to the forefront in more recent decades. Many professions have developed competency models, and there are numerous broad managerial and leadership competencies that have been identified by researchers, consultants, and assessment organizations. For example, there are many models for cybersecurity, project management, human resources management, accounting, and others. Models not specific to a profession include Lominger[2] and assessment models like Hogan.[3] One reason for the proliferation of competency models and lists of competencies is that they help to organize the behaviors that are needed by managers and for advancement into leadership positions. The best competency models are those that are carefully researched and updated regularly through additional research. The purpose of research to create competency models is to be able to distinguish between the most competent performers and mediocre or poor performers. In addition to identifying the behaviors of highly competent managers, competency models also serve as a guide for all managers in determining what they need to know and, more importantly, how they need to behave to be successful in their current and future roles. Understanding what is required is the first step to awareness of the talent, skill, and ability that is needed and which may or may not be possessed by an individual.

A competency is something measurable and, as a result, it is possible to identify what effective performance looks like compared to less effective performance. At this juncture, your focus is not on how to measure your competencies but rather to discuss how you can identify what competencies are important for you to know and how to determine which competencies will be necessary for personal development. Competency models tend to focus on the totality of what is needed in a profession or for a specific role or group of roles. Individual competencies, however, are skills that a manager can identify and work to develop on their own. For example, while there may be a competency model for managers in the hospitality industry or a medical field, the competency framework may have things that relate specifically to success in a hotel or a hospital. These models will also include general and transferable knowledge, skills, abilities, and other characteristics (KSAOs). Skills like communication, team-working, self-management, result-orientation, strategic-orientation, decision making, risk-taking, and creativity, can all have behavioral statements relative to the industry but also have general relevancy and behaviors that cut across all *industries* and many roles.

At the organizational level, without competencies, organizations would not have good insight into who to hire, promote, or develop. Competencies allow an organization to align values with performance and to identify expectations. Performance can and should be measured against competency expectations. Data such as this can guide succession planning and even more nuanced project assignments or can stretch goals. At the individual level, a focus on competencies can enable individuals to be proactive in their development and the roles they seek within the organization or industry.

Another key point is that competency needs change over time. Organizational priorities shift, reorganizations occur, and jobs are sometimes deconstructed and realigned based upon these changes. Likewise, as individuals advance or become involved with different projects or initiatives, their competency needs may change. A change in a boss or addition of staff to your team can also necessitate a different competency or proficiency level for specific competencies. For example, a manager who is an individual contributor, responsible for a program, may find themselves with direct reports if their role expands. If this is the case, they will need to develop their performance management, teamwork, perceptivity, and other skills.

Management Competencies

There are many different managerial competencies and quite a few models and configurations of relevant competencies. Table 2.1 is not an exhaustive list but is comprehensive in terms of the competencies needed by most managers today. This list[4] presents some common competencies that are often part of a competency framework or are considered both independently and interdependently, especially for developmental purposes. Competencies such as these can be clustered together. Additionally, some of the listed competencies can be further broken down into more granular skills. For example, teamwork could include building commitment, relationships, teams, and trust; whereas communication can also be broken down to oral, written, nonverbal, and listening skills.

Table 2.2 provides brief definitions for each of these competencies. This list forms the basis for self-assessment and examples throughout the book and guides the discussion of how to apply the learning tools and exercises provided. Management competencies are important because they serve as an outline of what you need to be able to do as a manager. They provide structure, just like any roadmap, to ensure that you get where you need to go and are effective along the journey.

Table 2.1 Important Management Competencies

1. Accountability	26. Initiative
2. Adaptability	27. Innovation
3. Analytical thinking	28. Interpersonal skills
4. Building relationships	29. Leadership
5. Building teams	30. Listening
6. Business acumen	31. Managing performance
7. Change management	32. Motivating
8. Coaching	33. Negotiation skills
9. Collaboration	34. Networking
10. Communication	35. Organization
11. Conflict management	36. Organization awareness
12. Continuous learning	37. Performance management
13. Creativity	38. Planning
14. Customer orientation	39. Presentation skills
15. Dealing with pressure	40. Problem-solving
16. Decision making	41. Project management
17. Delegating	42. Results orientation
18. Developing others	43. Risk-taking
19. Empowering others	44. Seeking/giving feedback
20. Ethics	45. Strategic thinking
21. Finance and budgeting	46. Stress management
22. Global mindset	47. Teamwork
23. Goal setting	48. Trust and respect
24. Human capital management	49. Valuing diversity
25. Influencing others	50. Work-life balance

Note: *This is not an exhaustive list; these 50 competencies are meant to provide you with a good sense of the various behavioral competencies that you are called upon to display effectively as a manager.*

Table 2.2 Defining Important Management Competencies

Accountability: accepts responsibility for tasks, assignments, and timeliness for completion and results.

Adaptability: flexibility and resilience to changing business needs and work assignments with employees, peers, supervisors, customers, and teams.

Analytical thinking: approaches problems with logic, systemic reasoning, and analysis of all problem components.

Building relationships: forming and sustaining strong connections with people inside and outside the organization.

Building teams: guiding, motivating, and sustaining groups of employees for maximum team effectiveness.

Business acumen: keen business sense; knowledge of business terms, functions to deal with business situations.

Change management: understands and enables the process of change; helps facilitate change with others.

Coaching: guiding employees to improvement by providing a future focus and helping to unlock potential.

(continued)

Table 2.2 (Cont.)

Collaboration: works with others as individuals or on teams to exchange ideas, partner, and cooperate.

Communication: giving, presenting, and exchanging information clearly, accurately, and in a timely fashion.

Conflict management: resolving complaints; settling disputes and helping to alleviate problems from escalating.

Continuous learning: focus on expanding skills and knowledge to build and maintain competence.

Creativity: inventiveness as applied to business situations to build value for team and organization.

Customer orientation: focus on the client, both internal and external satisfaction.

Dealing with pressure: balancing competing priorities in job, with boss, and in personal issues while maintaining effectiveness.

Decision making: choosing between options in a timely manner with high-quality outcomes.

Delegating: when appropriate, assigns responsibilities and tasks clearly to the right employees at the right time.

Developing others: actively cultivates staff through training, coaching, and assignments in a planful way.

Empowering others: showing confidence in and giving freedom to employees on tasks, goals, and resolving issues.

Ethics: dealing with good and evil and the principles that cover behavior from a moral perspective.

Finance and budgeting: understand financial and budgeting processes; manages to budget effectively.

Global mindset: aware of and open to different cultures across organizations and cultures; works cross-culturally.

Goal setting: establishing realistic and specific goals; then staying on target to meet goals regardless of the situation or adjusting as necessary to accommodate new circumstances.

Human capital management: recruits, develops, and retains workforce as appropriate in a variety of situations.

Influencing others: earning support from others; adapting style for sway and impact.

Initiative: seizing opportunities; proactive in dealing with problems or possibilities promptly and actively.

Innovation: uses and values creative and novel ideas to solve problems or meet organizational goals.

Interpersonal skills: effectively relating to others; helps others to feel appreciated, valued, and understood.

Leadership: directing, guiding, and influencing others to be motivated, accomplish goals, and feel a sense of order.

Listening: active attention to others; seeks to understand, elicits feedback, and hears all points of view.

Managing performance: effectively manages achievement or production; intervenes as necessary, provides feedback.

Table 2.2 (Cont.)

Motivating: inspires others to accomplish goals or tasks – even if no direct reporting relationship exists; knows what drives people in different situations.

Negotiation skills: listening and collaborating to find an outcome that maintains trust and positive relationships.

Networking: connecting and maintaining relationships with others to further organizational and personal goals.

Organization: planning and systematizing effectively for self and others; prioritizes, schedules, and leverages resources.

Organization awareness: conscious of organization's goals, priorities, vision, culture, and values; incorporates recognition into actions.

Performance management: helps to set accurate goals, assess achievement, and provide effective/timely feedback.

Planning: gathers input, sets realistic goals and schedules with measurable milestones; includes contingency planning.

Presentation skills: delivers ideas and information effectively to groups or individuals; adapts to different audiences.

Problem-solving: resolves problems by accurately evaluating issues, resources, and timing; assesses complexity, weighs options, and finds effective solutions.

Project management: planning, organizing, and executing all the activities and resource needs associated with a temporary initiative.

Results orientation: outcome orientation; identifies what needs to be done and focuses efforts to achieve desired outcomes consistent with objectives.

Risk-taking: evaluates actions to achieve positive outcomes when the potential for negative consequences exist.

Seeking/giving feedback: clarifies, comments, and explains to help others be successful; solicits same for self; coaches and applies feedback to achieve goals.

Strategic thinking: considers long-term interests by considering internal and external factors; applies analysis.

Stress management: maintains demeanor; maintains effectiveness under pressure; adapts and develops strategies to deal with the strain.

Teamwork: cooperates and works collaboratively with others to achieve coordination and reach goals.

Trust and respect: supports others and operates with integrity providing confidence in their integrity; gains confidence and regard of stakeholders.

Valuing diversity: establishes and maintains a work environment in which people from diverse backgrounds feel included and valued.

Work-life balance: maintains stability between personal and work needs achieving harmony between the responsibilities of each.

Proficiency Levels

One of the helpful things about competencies, particularly for personal development, is that examples of behavior can be broken down into proficiency levels – in other words, how good is your skill? Building trust, for instance, can be broken down into four or five descriptors that range from high proficiency to very low proficiency. Levels such as these often aid in the assessment of where an employee is on the continuum with an eye toward the development of where you want the performance to grow. As an example, building trust might have five levels ranging from:

1. **Excellent** standing for trustworthiness and integrity
2. **Very good** standing for trustworthiness and integrity
3. **Good** standing for trustworthiness and integrity
4. **Developing** standing for trustworthiness and integrity
5. **Poor** standing for trustworthiness and integrity

Another way to view proficiency levels, particularly from a developmental perspective rather than an evaluative perspective, is to think of the levels as:

1. Novice
2. Foundational
3. Intermediate
4. Advanced
5. Expert

Or, if you wanted a 4-point scale rather than a 5-point scale:

1. Basic
2. Intermediate
3. Advanced
4. Expert

Regardless of whether you use a 4-point or 5-point continuum of levels, the idea is that behavioral statements can be created for each level and distinguish levels of performance. Depending upon where an individual falls on the proficiency continuum, goals can be developed for learning or experience opportunities to assist in achieving higher levels of performance. Chapter 4, Self-assessment, offers a proficiency level continuum that can be used for assessing your proficiency levels for each competency.

Managers require a wide range of cognitive and technical skills to be effective in their role. These skills are translated into the day-to-day behaviors that customers, peers, subordinates, and those in senior positions see. It is often the case that managers are sent to formal training programs that are offered either internally or externally. While these programs can be quite helpful, they are sometimes so focused on the topic as to miss the everyday opportunity of learning through self-development. Further, it is essential to note that there should be no expectation that individuals be highly proficient in all competencies immediately or simultaneously. This is a development process that must take place such that you consider what you need now versus the future. Keep in mind that some competencies may be like muscles; if you don't use them for a while, it may take exercise and practice to restore them to previous proficiency levels. If it's been a while since you used a particular competency, you may not be as proficient as you once were in that competency.

Value of Developing Competencies Beyond Technical Expertise

Technical expertise is important to any manager. It provides a foundation upon which your managerial career is built. However, technical expertise is not what allows you to be a good manager. Technical competency demonstrates your knowledge, skill, and ability in a particular discipline or profession. Managerial competency is what enables you to be effective in applying your technical competency and in managing others. Without the skills and abilities in the competencies listed in Table 2.1, an excellent technical expert may fail as a manager. When someone studies an engineering discipline in college or goes into training to be an electrician, they often learn specialized knowledge about their field and may not learn how to organize, lead, or direct the work of others. Proficient technical experts are frequently promoted for their technical expertise and often put in situations where they are not prepared to manage programs and people. This is not to take away from the expertise that allowed them to be promoted, but to underscore that, in some cases, it is a recipe for ineffectiveness if not a failure as a manager.

Sometimes it takes a while for managers to understand how important their behavioral skills are compared to their technical expertise. The challenge, of course, is that new managers, and even seasoned managers, often do not know the impact they have on others and where their strengths and weaknesses lie. Managers, over time, are usually doing less and less in their technical field and more and more under the broad umbrella of managing. They may be focusing on many, if not all, of the competencies that are listed and defined in Table 2.2.

Time and Need Orientation Framework

To develop managerial proficiency in the competencies needed to be successful, it is important to think in terms of both your time orientation and need orientation. For the sake of simplicity, think of time orientation as being either current or future-focused. What is it that you need now to be successful in your current role? What will you need to advance and thrive in the future? From a need perspective, you can think of personal needs compared to professional requirements. What is it that you need to be effective in living your day-to-day life compared to what you need to be successful in your role as an employee in an organization? In reality, there may be additional layers of time or need orientation, but, for context, a two-by-two is ample. Figure 2.1 shows the two-by-two time and need framework that can be applied to any manager or individual. Example 2.1 depicts a hypothetical example of a two-by-two framework with some key competencies highlighted.

In the example, it is clear that there may be overlap in personal and professional needs. Competency development, while different in orientation, may be needed and useful in both areas. There may also be an overlap in current and future needs. For example, a person may need to develop their decision making skills now

	Current Orientation	Future Orientation
Personal Needs		
Professional Needs		

Figure 2.1 Time and Need Orientation Framework

Example 2.1 General Example – Time and Need Orientation Framework

	Current Orientation	Future Orientation
Personal Needs	• **Interpersonal skills** to meet and maintain friendships. • **Self-confidence** to complete a degree or certification. • **Decision making** to determine preferences on where to live and in selecting friends.	• **Accountability** to ensure all obligations are met. • **Stress management** to safeguard against burnout and health issues. • **Organization** – to juggle personal obligations.
Professional Needs	• **Interpersonal skills** to interact with coworkers in a tactful manner. • **Listening** through attention to detail and incorporating input. • **Networking** by seeking opportunities to create professional connections.	• **Stress management** in order to cope with change and increased responsibility. • **Collaboration** by working with others across boundaries. • **Results** orientation by focusing on an outcome and what it takes to achieve the outcome.

concerning the issues they face today, but in the future, the complexity of what they need may be far more significant. As a result, competency development in the future may look quite different and involve much more diversity and sophistication concerning learning.

If you're reading this book, it is likely because you want to be a better manager, or, because you'd like to help your staff be better managers. There are countless books on how to be a better manager. Some focus on a specific aspect of management, while others focus on management in general. The reality is that developing your managerial competence is something that takes place over time and, in many ways, never ends. The key question is where to start and how to maintain your focus. It's easy to identify things like "provide greater feedback" or "set clear goals," but these tips focus on things to do rather than developing your skills in a way that resonates best with you. Becoming an effective manager requires a great deal of observation, growth, and self-awareness. The skills that you gain to win a position are not necessarily the skills that you need to advance in an organization. Assuming that once you've learned a particular set of skills, you don't need to continue developing those same skills or adding new ones is a critical mistake in terms of management development.

Developing Competencies for Success

Every person is unique, and while titles may sometimes be the same, every job is different. We can, however, identify some similarities between people and jobs concerning how they approach their development and from what career orientation they hail. Consider the following three managers – all in need of development yet all in a different place in their career journey and competency needs.

Dara: Middle Manager

Dara is a middle manager who has an undergraduate degree in business and works in an IT-related field with seven direct reports. Her job keeps her busy with meetings, scheduling, and the like. She desires to advance in her organization and move into senior management. Dara has received very positive reviews and is thought of as a highly competent manager in her day-to-day role. Dara has come to realize that if she wants to ascend to senior management, she will need to develop some of her existing competencies and attain additional competencies to which she has had little to no exposure in her career to date. Specifically, while Dara is strong in tactical areas and in executing plans, she's had little experience with strategic thinking and global mindsets.

Dara has a strong desire to be self-directed to work on developing the competencies needed to advance her career. Working in IT, Dara's day is often meeting after meeting or crisis after crisis where she is called on to put out fires or solve immediate problems. How, thought Dara, can she gain the experience and expertise needed to be noticed as someone who can also be competent in roles that require competence in areas to which she has no access? On a personal note, Dara is married with two young children and also has some caregiving responsibilities for her dad, who lives in the same city. Using the time and need orientation framework, Example 2.2 is what Dara may be facing.

Example 2.2 Dara – Middle Manager

	Current Orientation	Future Orientation
Personal Needs	• Decision making • Planning • Listening	• Negotiation skills • Change management • Delegating
Professional Needs	• Accountability • Managing performance • Customer orientation • Problem-solving	• Strategic thinking • Global mindset • Building relationships • Finance and budgeting

Nick: Individual Contributor

Nick is a relatively new manager. Although the word "manager" is in his title, he's an individual contributor and does not supervise others. Nick has an under-graduate degree in industrial engineering and, after a few years of work, went back to school to obtain his MBA, which he just completed (while working full-time) a few months ago. Nick's eyes were opened in graduate school when he learned a bit more about leadership, organizational behavior, and management. Nick is well versed in all things technical, but until his MBA, he had little knowledge, skill, or ability in the behavioral side of working.

Nick is a robotics manager and spends much of his day researching and testing. Part of the reason for obtaining his MBA was so that he could use his technical foundation as a springboard for a leadership position, or perhaps to become an entrepreneur. Now that he has more time, since he's no longer taking classes, writing papers, and studying, he would like to better prepare himself for the lead-ership roles to which he aspires. On a personal note, Nick is single and hoping to start a family in the next few years. He moved to a new city to start this job and shortly after that started his MBA at night. He's made some friends from the MBA program but has not devoted much time to socialize into the broader community. Example 2.3 is what Nick's journey may look like.

Chris: Senior Manager

Chris is a senior manager who has enjoyed a long and varied career. Most of Chris's time, almost 20 years, has been spent in the same organization in the same location. Promotions over time have led to the current senior position. Two weeks ago, the rug was pulled out from under Chris when it was announced that the company had been sold and would be merging with a much larger multinational company. Chris has been successful due to hard work, loyalty, and being an all-around good manager and technical expert. It's become quite apparent to Chris that times are about to change. The relaxed family culture that has been ever-present in the organization will, out of necessity and natural evolution, be changing.

In the past 20 years, all of Chris's development has been through traditional sources such as conferences, workshops, and seminars. Chris fears that the things

Example 2.3 Nick – Individual Contributor

	Current Orientation	Future Orientation
Personal Needs	• Teamwork • Work–life balance • Collaboration	• Work–life balance • Initiative • Adaptability
Professional Needs	• Continuous learning • Business acumen • Seeking/giving feedback	• Leadership • Seek/give feedback • Negotiation

Example 2.4 Chris – Senior Manager

	Current Orientation	**Future Orientation**
Personal Needs	• Accountability • Initiative • Results orientation	• Change management • Trust and respect • Adaptability
Professional Needs	• Goal setting • Organization awareness • Teamwork	• Change management • Presentation skills • Influencing others • Initiative

which need to be learned will not come directly from courses, instructors, or books. How, thought Chris, will this development unfold? On a personal note, Chris is a "hometown" individual who enjoys the comfort of lots of local friends and family. Vacations typically don't take the family too far away, and that's just fine with Chris. Example 2.4 is what Chris may be facing.

Each of these three managers is at somewhat of a crossroad in their career. It is likely that each has had a different learning journey. It is also likely that each is internally motivated to prepare for their next career chapter. Going forward, each of these managers will take a self-directed development approach to learning – in addition to any traditional training they may get from their respective organizations. We will revisit the stories of Dara, Nick, and Chris throughout Chapters 5 through 9, to illustrate how individuals can apply self-directed learning activities to help them develop the managerial behaviors they need to be successful.

Competencies, like the ones defined in Table 2.2, can all be researched, discussed, and studied in libraries and training programs. They can, and also should, be a target of self-directed learning. The next two chapters will explore self-directed learning and self-assessment.

Notes

1 www.workforce.com/2002/09/03/31-core-competencies-explained/; www.amanet. org/resources/success-skills/management/; www.ccl.org/articles/leading-effectively-articles/6-skills-middle-level-leaders-need/; www.inc.com/peter-economy/top-10-skills-every-great-leader-needs-to-succeed.html

2 www.quora.com/What-are-the-67-Lominger-Competencies-1

3 https://www.hoganassessments.com/

4 List of competencies developed from a variety of sources, including, but not limited to: http://hr.babson.edu/competencies/competencypdfs/competencieswithproficiencylevels.pdf, www.opm.gov/policy-data-oversight/assessment-and-selection/competencies/proficiency-levels-for-leadership-competencies.pdf, www.kipp.org/wp-content/uploads/2016/11/KIPP_Leadership_Competency_Model.pdf; www.quora.com/What-are-the-67-Lominger-Competencies-1

Bibliography

American Management Association (Retrieved June, 2019). Skills for Managers and Leaders. Available: www.amanet.org/resources/success-skills/management/

Babson (Retrieved July, 2019). Competency Descriptions & Proficiency Levels. Available: http://hr.babson.edu/competencies/competencypdfs/competencieswithproficiencyle vels.pdf

Center for Creative Leadership (Retrieved May, 2019). 6 Key Skills Leaders in the Middle Need to Advance. Available: www.ccl.org/articles/leading-effectively-articles/6-skills-middle-level-leaders-need/

Cripe, E. (2002). 31 Core Competencies Explained. Available: www.workforce.com/2002/09/03/31-core-competencies-explained/

Economy, P. (Retrieved June, 2019). Top 10 Skills Every Great Leader Needs to Succeed. *Inc.* Available: www.inc.com/peter-economy/top-10-skills-every-great-leader-needs-to-succeed.html

Hogan (Retrieved June, 2019). Hogan Leadership Forecast Series. Available: www.performanceprograms.com/self-assessments/leadership-effectiveness/hogan-leadership-forecast-series/

KIPP (Retrieved June, 2019). KIPP: Leadership Framework and Competency Model. Available: www.kipp.org/wp-content/uploads/2016/11/KIPP_Leadership_Competency_Model.pdf

U.S. Office of Personnel Management (Retrieved June, 2019). Proficiency Levels for Leadership Competencies. Available: www.opm.gov/policy-data-oversight/assessment-and-selection/competencies/proficiency-levels-for-leadership-competencies.pdf

Wilsbacher, J. (2017). What are the 67 Lominger Competencies? Available: www.quora.com/What-are-the-67-Lominger-Competencies-1

3 Self-directed Learning

Self-directed learning is a process in which people take the initiative, with or without the help of others, in identifying learning needs, formulating learning goals, identifying resources for active learning, then selecting and applying appropriate mechanisms to facilitate learning.[1] This means that the individual is taking responsibility for all aspects of learning and development. Self-directed learning does not mean that learning activities are done solely by yourself, nor does it mean that all activities are decided on and executed without assistance. The learner typically owns the final decision regarding who is involved, what is done, when, and how. Self-directed learners are typically self-motivated, tend to be persistent, are independent, are usually self-disciplined, set their goals and remain goal oriented, and develop more self-confidence over time. This last point is critical for managers who need and want to improve their managerial and behavioral skills.

What is self-directed learning? How can managers at all levels develop management competencies on their own? How does a manager become a self-directed learner? How can you sustain self-directed learning? What are the strategies to be a successful self-directed learner? What are the advantages of self-directed learning? How can self-directed learning be used as a professional development tool for managers? Can self-directed learning become a way of life to ensure future success? This chapter explores the answers to these questions.

Self-directed learning can mean no structure, no teacher or facilitator, no curriculum or goals. Alternatively, it can be the exact opposite! That is, self-directed learning is multifaceted, flexible, and is a process by which an individual takes the initiative to create a learning plan or experience for themselves that will meet their needs and motivate them to achieve success. According to Gibbons,[2] "self-directed learning is any knowledge, skill, accomplishment, or personal development that an individual chooses and brings about by his or her efforts using any method in any circumstance at any time." This definition resonates because it shows the sheer versatility of self-directed learning. In short, it is what the learner wants it to be, but at the core, it is directional and purpose-driven for the development of knowledge, skills, abilities, and other characteristics (KSAOs).

Modern theorists suggest that self-directed learning is a process of "authentic control" where the learner sorts through their own experiences to understand the meaning of what they've learned.[3] Brookfield[4] suggests two essential characteristics. First, that self-direction is the continuous exercise by the learner of authentic control over all decisions to do with learning. Second, that self-direction is the ability to gain access to, and choose from, a full range of available and appropriate resources. People who have learned a subject on their own, without the direct benefit of a teacher or master craft person, are called autodidacts.[5]

Most of us, whether we realize it or not, spend much time gaining new skills and information. Sometimes this occurs in a formal planned way, but quite often it happens somewhat informally. The pace of change today is, or at least feels, more rapid than in the past. As a result, we need to acquire new knowledge and skills. Most of us take the initiative on some level to read books and articles, or to search the Internet for some piece of information we need or want. However, when was the last time you had a specific plan to learn something for which you did a self-assessment or built a program of specific self-study? That is, when have you taken responsibility, on your own, to learn something for development purposes through your means rather than through formal training or education? To understand how, when, and why we should take this responsibility, let's first look at adult learning.

Adult Learning

As managers and employees, we have an abundance of available and appropriate resources open to us regularly. The premise of this book is that we should all avail ourselves of these resources and moreover, that when we apply some structure, through mechanisms like role playing, observation, questions, and so forth, our learning will be all the richer and more effective. Brookfield[6] argues that the nature of the self in self-directed learning is that learning is a social activity. Moreover, "self" in the learning process is culturally formed. As a result, the application of self-directed learning may differ from region to region. This, of course, has implications for managers from other countries or who are working globally. The assumption of adult learning is that we don't all need to be autodidacts and teach ourselves an entire subject but we can be self-aware and autonomous in our learning efforts to build our skills.

An essential foundation of adult learning states that "experience is the richest source for adult learning."[7] This is the key because experience isn't just something that one encounters; it is something that you can create with intention. Another foundation is that an adult's orientation to learning is "life-centered." Although this may seem to state the obvious, it is important because of its pragmatism. There is an air of practicality to this aspect of adult learning that makes self-directed learning especially prudent and feasible.[8] One challenge is that a person's life situation today may or may not reflect the life situation of tomorrow, for which you need to prepare. Nonetheless, planning for needs in advance creates focus and structure and makes learning goals attainable.

Adult learning theory essentially asserts that adults learn differently from children and even college-aged students. Adult learning theory, often called andragogy, emphasizes that adults:[9]

- must want to learn
- need a variety of learning methods
- want to know why they need to learn something
- learn by doing – experiencing
- want to participate actively in the learning process
- are very goal-directed and, in fact, self-directed
- take responsibility for the planning and execution of learning activities
- must acknowledge past experiences and the role they play in their learning

Given these foundational statements regarding adult learning, it is reasonable to assume that every adult may approach learning a bit differently and that your propensity for self-directed learning may fall on a continuum from basic to advanced. Figure 3.1 depicts this continuum. At a basic level, which most people display, there is curiosity followed by searching for and reading information. At the intermediate level, the self-directed learner is more deliberate. A person in this level creates some structure, asks a lot of questions, looks for and recognizes learning opportunities, begins to apply what they learn and may engage others to assist. At the advanced level, the self-directed learner will be very purposeful and intentional. A learning *plan* will be created and the learner will drive and adapt the agenda as needed.

How self-directed are you? Where on the continuum do you think you fall? Are you self-directed in some things but not others? Worksheet 3.1 provides an exercise to help you to assess where on the self-directed learning continuum you may sit. Self-directed learning is something that you can influence and get better at over time.

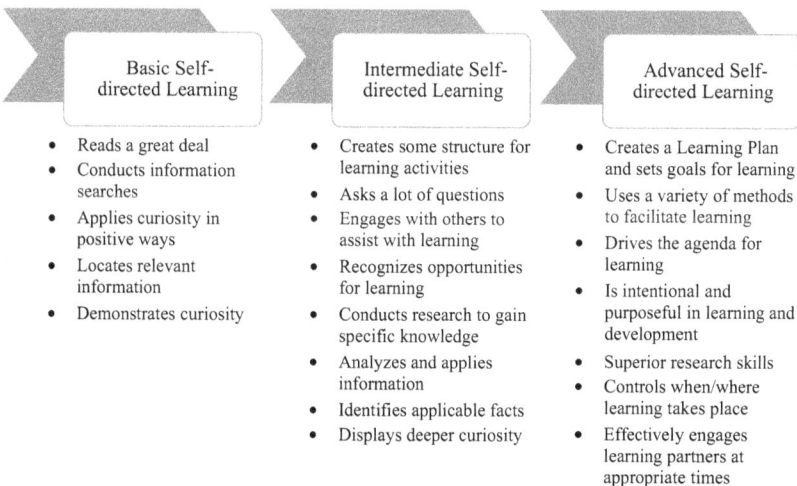

Basic Self-directed Learning	Intermediate Self-directed Learning	Advanced Self-directed Learning
• Reads a great deal • Conducts information searches • Applies curiosity in positive ways • Locates relevant information • Demonstrates curiosity	• Creates some structure for learning activities • Asks a lot of questions • Engages with others to assist with learning • Recognizes opportunities for learning • Conducts research to gain specific knowledge • Analyzes and applies information • Identifies applicable facts • Displays deeper curiosity	• Creates a Learning Plan and sets goals for learning • Uses a variety of methods to facilitate learning • Drives the agenda for learning • Is intentional and purposeful in learning and development • Superior research skills • Controls when/where learning takes place • Effectively engages learning partners at appropriate times

Figure 3.1 Self-directed Learning Continuum

Worksheet 3.1 Are You a Self-directed Learner?

Instructions: Place a check mark in the column that you think is the right assessment of your agreement to the statements on the left. Be as realistic and accurate as possible. Remember, no one needs to see this but you.

	Strongly Agree	Agree	Not Sure	Disagree	Strongly Disagree
I am curious.					
If I don't know something, I look it up.					
I am goal-directed.					
I understand that learning takes discipline.					
I want to develop my skills and behaviors.					
I know I can develop a plan for learning.					
I am reasonably self-aware of my skills and abilities.					
I challenge myself to find learning opportunities in a variety of ways.					
I am open to learning from others – with or without their help.					
I am comfortable asking others for feedback/input.					
I see problems as challenges rather than as obstacles.					
I am self-motivated.					
I can see learning opportunities just about anywhere.					
I think being prepared to learn is essential.					
I believe in practicing to get better at something.					
I know I can learn from others.					
If I create a plan, I stick to it.					
I think I can learn through observation.					
I believe that asking the right questions is essential for learning.					

Worksheet 3.1 (Cont.)

	Strongly Agree	Agree	Not Sure	Disagree	Strongly Disagree
I think taking notes and writing things down helps me to learn.					
I organize my time well.					
I like to learn.					
I prefer to develop a plan to guide my learning.					
I like looking for information.					

Interpretation: There is no score to this self-assessment. For the items that you marked Disagree or Strongly Disagree, try to understand why this is the case. Prepare bullet points for each to analyze your reluctance to engage in the learning behavior listed. The fewer things with which you disagree, the more open you are likely to be to learning on your own.

Characteristics of Self-directed Learners

Self-directed learners are successful when they exhibit self-motivation, self-reliance, and when they can reflect on and honestly assess their progress and approach. While it may be tempting to think that these characteristics are only innate, in many instances, the attributes of self-directed learners can be developed and honed over time. An individual can decide to cast a wide net for relevant learning, be future-focused, be organized, and commit to personal and professional development. While some may have more of a natural proclivity to self-directed learning than others, these are behaviors that can be learned and practiced. Table 3.1 shows a list of the characteristics that are typically present in the self-directed learner.

This is a long list of characteristics and qualities. Don't be alarmed if you don't feel that all these characteristics describe who you are today as a learner. Some of this may come from within, such as self-motivation or curiosity, but most of these qualities can be learned and developed so that self-directed learning becomes part of who you are and how you approach your responsibilities as a learner. Self-directed learning can be viewed in and of itself as a competency. Moreover, competencies, as we know, are abilities which can be groomed and developed.

Face-to-face Learning Compared to Self-directed Learning

Adult learners are those who are typically engaged in something other than learning as a full-time focus. For example, the adult learner may be working or volunteering and has a desire to learn something they think will be useful. We know that self-directed learning is learning that the individual brings about by themselves. We also know that self-directed learning can be distinguished from more traditional face-to-face learning in multiple ways. With self-directed learning, there's more control

Table 3.1 Characteristics of Self-directed Learners

• Ambitious	• Genuinely interested in learning
• Awareness of self and learning needs	• Goal oriented
• Career-minded	• Good at engaging others in their learning
• Cast a wide net for relevant learning	• Intentional
• Committed to personal development	• Mindful of the present
• Control their learning experiences	• Organizes time and effort well
• Curious	• Reflective of self and learning
• Determined to achieve success	• Resourceful
• Develops a learning plan	• Self-motivated
• Driven by self	• Self-reliant
• Dynamic	• Self-starting
• Energetic	• Sets their own pace for learning
• Enjoys learning	• Successful
• Future-focused	• Takes initiative

and direction from the learner whereas with conventional face-to-face education the direction and control typically come from an external source.

Traditional face-to-face learning tends to be classroom-based and directed by an instructor and an agenda. Participants may or may not be motivated depending upon why they are attending the course or if they were told to attend versus asking to attend training. The pace is set by the instructor and the agenda typically does not change – regardless of the range of knowledge and skills that are possessed by the learners in the room. Face-to-face learning can be effective and useful but may vary from participant to participant. Self-directed learning, on the other hand, tends to be driven by "self" rather than others. The objectives and pace are set by the learner and are tied to the individual's knowledge, skill, ability, and objectives for learning. Self-directed learning may include attending outside learning or face-to-face learning, but this is part of a larger plan that is driven by and customized for the learner. Table 3.2 provides the contrast of traditional face-to-face learning compared to self-directed learning.

There are many benefits to self-directed learning. First and perhaps most significant is the fact that self-directed learning teaches a person how to learn as opposed to what to learn. With the skill of self-directed learning, a person can be a lifelong purposeful learner. The independence a person has with self-directed learning provides the tools for application, practice, and realism. Besides the freedom to choose what to learn, when, and how to learn, self-directed learning also motivates people to seek a variety of learning approaches and situations. Ultimately, self-directed learning can increase a person's self-confidence, communication skills, and overall performance by helping to shape behaviors.

Steps for Self-directed Learning

To better understand self-directed learning let's explore the steps that can be taken to create a self-directed learning approach, resulting in a plan for learning. There

Table 3.2 Face-to-face Learning Compared to Self-directed Learning

Face-to-face Learning	Self-directed Learning
• Classroom-based	• Individuals take the initiative to learn
• Lecture and group exercise based	• Learner manages own time
• Structured agenda with live interaction; instructor setting pace	• Self-paced
	• Learner drives the agenda
• Uses prepared material designed for training or education curriculum	• Learner controls when/where learning takes place
• Learners may request to participate or could be told to attend	• The learner conducts self-assessment
• Learners may or may not be motivated	• Learners are curious and motivated – often driven
• Learners may or may not understand the need to participate	• Learners ask many questions
	• Self-directed learning may occur anytime, anywhere
• Learning is always with the help of others	• Learning is with or without the help of others
• Trainer/instructor controls the agenda	• There may be no "end" for a specific learning objective
• Learning is usually structured and may not account for individual needs	• Learner chooses the study material
• Other learners are present; they may or may not be at the same level of need	• The learner can choose to engage others for assistance with learning
• A relationship exists between fellow learners and the instructor for learning	• The learner can choose to incorporate formal training or education into the learning plan
• Allows for expression and nonverbal behavior to add context for learners	

are six steps that managers can follow to create a self-directed learning approach. Following these six steps to effective self-directed learning need not be limiting or restrictive. Being an independent learner offers flexibility and control. After you've developed a learning plan once (or twice) for a competency you want to build, the flow and ease of the steps will be smooth and something that can be done quickly – either formally or informally. The process begins with self-assessment and then moves to a consideration of your readiness to learn. Based on these two steps, goals are created followed by a learning plan. The final two steps are execution of the plan, concluding with evaluation and reassessment. Figure 3.2 depicts the steps in the process.

Step One: Self-assessment

To be self-directed, you must first know what learning is needed and you must be self-aware. You may be very good at what you do already, and as discussed in Chapter 2 you may have different needs now than in the future. Regardless of the impetus, you should complete a self-assessment. The purpose of this first step is to be clear about what you want to accomplish by knowing what you can and can't do and by honestly assessing your strengths and weaknesses on skills that you need. Self-assessments will be covered in more detail in Chapter 4.

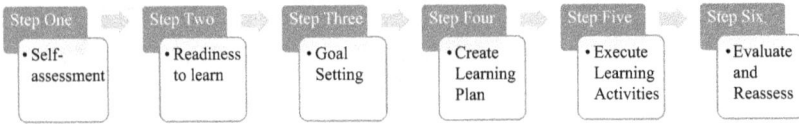

Figure 3.2 Six-step Process for Self-directed Learning

Step Two: Readiness to Learn

Readiness to learn relates to the theory of adult learning and the fact that adults must want to learn, see the need to learn, and be open to the learning experience. This can be both straightforward and complex. Straightforward in that the tenets of adult learning indicate that a person's attitude and openness to learning are critical for learning to take place. Complex in that willingness to learn is dependent on many factors in an individual's environment – both work and personal.

The self-directed learning assessment in Worksheet 3.1 shows that many factors contribute to whether or not a person is a self-directed learner. However, the exercise does not address where a person may be at any given time concerning their mindset for learning. For example, if work is particularly busy, if there is a significant transition occurring, or if there is a change in key staff that a person reports to or who report up, then the work environment may not be ideal for the focus that is needed to be successful with self-directed learning. On the other hand, it may be that this is *precisely* the time when learning would be the greatest. Still, readiness must be felt by the learner. Receptivity may be the difference between whether learning is internalized and transferred to the workplace or not. Attention to personal factors must be considered as well. For example, marriage, children, caregiving, volunteer activities, and a host of other individual factors may influence whether a person feels as though they have the capacity to take on a learning journey.

Readiness to learn, like dieting or following an exercise regimen, can't be forced. The learner, dieter, or exerciser must be willing and inclined to follow the plan. Developing a plan and setting goals are in some respects the easy part. The good news is that the approach in this book is for everyone, irrespective of whether they have a considerable amount of time to focus on learning. The intent is that learning can coincide with important personal and professional agenda items and be accomplished while being successful in your existing role. A realistic course of action must be taken. Goals and plans need to fit with the learner's mindset and attitude.

Step Three: Goal Setting

Goal setting is one of the most robust motivation theories that exists.[10] The reason is simple. Goal setting works. To the degree that goals are specific, measurable, and represent a stretch for the individual, they can be quite motivating. It is widely known that the more specific and realistic your goals and the clearer your expectations, the greater likelihood there is to accomplish the goals. For self-directed learning to work, the learner must identify a goal or set of goals that they wish to achieve through the learning plan. This will enable a structure to be created and a plan to be built. There can be a single goal or multiple goals depending upon what level of need exists, or what time and focus the learner thinks can be given.

If the competency a manager wishes to develop is "delegating," what might a goal look like for this learning journey? A goal "to be better at delegating" is not likely to be as motivating and directional as a goal "to identify where in each direct report's job delegation is possible and delegate to each direct report at least once a week." Moreover, this overriding goal for delegation may lead to a whole subset of goals or components to a learning plan. For example, the following goals could materialize when applying the goal-setting process to developing a delegation competency:

1. Learn what delegation is and how to accomplish delegation.
2. Understand why delegation is not done and why people shy away from the effort.
3. Identify tasks and assignments within the scope of my responsibility that can be articulated and given to one or more direct reports.
4. Identify my barriers preventing delegation.
5. Learn how others are successful in delegation.
6. Develop skills in explaining task assignments and allowing direct reports to complete assignments independently without micromanaging.
7. Understand what resources and time employees need to be given to complete delegated assignments.
8. Delegate at least once per week to each direct report during the first month and at least twice per month thereafter.

The application of goal setting is versatile. You can develop a long list like the one above and you can break it down so you have goals by the day, week, or month. The goals are up to the learner and the key is in having them clearly articulated and then following them.

Step Four: Create Learning Plan

Once you have set your goals for learning it is essential to establish a plan for accomplishing the goals. First, think about how to prioritize the goals; it may be that learning certain skills will be the foundation for others. It may also be that specific goals will rank higher on your list of things to accomplish than others. Creating a sequence for your goals will also allow you to build in structure concerning the type and timing of your learning. Creating a timeline for completion as part of the plan will also be important. It is possible to focus on more than one goal at a time as there may be overlap in your learning opportunities or activities. However, establishing a realistic time frame for completion will have the same value as setting goals because it will help to keep momentum for learning and keep the education process moving.

In addition to the timeline for completing goals, it will be essential to identify the resources and materials you will need to accomplish the learning that is desired. To illustrate, using the example of delegating, the following activities may be part of the learning plan:

- Week 1: Research articles and materials about effective delegation.
- Week 1: Develop a list of questions and concepts to explore.
- Week 2: Set up meetings with fellow managers both inside and outside of the company.
- Week 2: Begin observing others delegating effectively; follow up with others as appropriate to get additional information.
- Week 3: Identify tasks that you currently do and want to delegate. Identify staff to whom you wish to delegate the tasks.
- Week 3: Ask a colleague or friend to help you practice delegating by engaging in a role play scenario.
- Week 3: Start with one direct report and delegate an assignment. Assuming this goes well, continue the practice and delegate more tasks to other staff.

This is a sample timeline, and it is entirely possible that the process could take less time if you've already been delegating small things and are trying to advance to a higher level or more complex delegation. It could, however, take more time if you've just been promoted to a manager role and you have not had any practice at delegation. As part of the plan, you will want to be specific for things like whom you will observe, whom you will engage in asking about delegation strategies, and whom you will ask to assist with a role play. Besides, you will want to match up employees with the task assignments you've earmarked for delegation. The more specific you can be the better the plan is as a guideline to follow. More discussion on how to create an overall development plan will be covered at the end of Chapter 4.

Step Five: Execute Learning Plan

Decide when to start your learning plan and replace the "week" notation in the plan with actual dates. Make sure that you start the plan when you are confident that you can stay reasonably close to your timeline. If there is a significant event or complicating factors such as a major deadline, holidays, or vacations, think about when the best time will be to initiate the process. Follow up on the milestones you set and the subgoals to ensure that you are meeting the expectations that you've set. Gauge whether or not your timeline remains realistic and if the goals themselves are a good fit and representative of what you need to learn. As you execute and learn more, it is possible that you will find the goals you created are not all on point or that there is something else you need to add or postpone. A learning plan can be fluid and is meant as a motivator to keep your learning on track. Keep in mind that executing a learning plan needs to be fit in with performing your job. While you do want to maintain your momentum, it may be necessary to adjust your timeline to take into consideration work requirements.

Step Six: Evaluate and Reassess

At the end of the defined learning process, or when you think your skill has reached the desired proficiency, take time to go back and judge how successful the *process* was and if your goals are met. Measure your completion rate for goals and do an appraisal of what you learned and how well you followed the process. Because this is a self-directed process, you will want to incorporate what you have learned about the goal-setting process and the sequence of activities you've chosen in future learning plans. You will find that over time you become more efficient and effective at setting goals, establishing timelines, and executing your plan.

At this stage, you may be asking yourself how (or when) do I know if I've learned enough? There is no instructor and probably no supervisor looking over your shoulder to provide specific feedback or to place a checkmark beside each milestone. Also, if you're very curious and like to keep learning it may be difficult to "turn off" the go switches on your learning for a particular competency. To make progress and continue with your overarching objective of competency development you will need to move on and avoid getting stuck in a particular area. Remember that while you may deem yourself successful in completing a learning plan, there is no reason why you can't keep an open eye and ear for learning. For example, if three months after you've executed and evaluated your learning plan for delegation you watch another manager masterfully handle a difficult delegation, you can easily incorporate this learning into your repertoire. In some ways, a completed process is never fully concluded. Like the dieter who achieves a desired weight loss, you can never totally lose your focus on your ultimate weight goal.

Self-directed Learning and Professional Development

Self-directed learning in the context of professional development can be explained by looking at the employer perspective compared to the employee perspective. When you consider the employee perspective versus the employer perspective, there is an inverse relationship between what the organization provides compared to what an individual can do on their own. There is a hierarchical structure to learning in terms of who directs or controls the learning.

At the bottom of the pyramid, there are everyday development activities that an organization may provide or offer to employees in pursuit of professional development. For example, conferences or workshops typically offer good content, but it is content that is directed and planned for an audience that will include learners who may be on very different learning journeys from one another in terms of how much they know or what they want to learn. These organized events and learning interventions are planned with one audience in mind and typically do not account for individual differences. At the top of the pyramid, independent and self-directed learning is in many ways the opposite. Here, the learner is attempting to reach their full potential and self-actualization. Maslow, who based much of his need hierarchy on the work of Goldstein, talked about self-actualization as a goal.

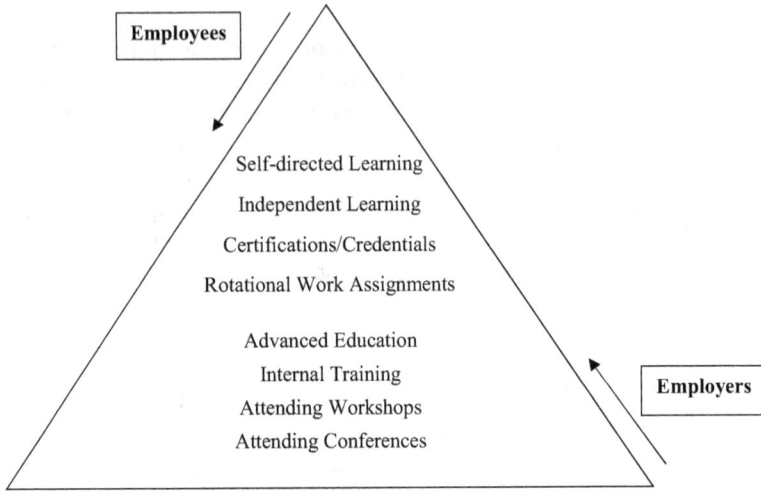

Figure 3.3 Self-directed Learning Hierarchy

The two theorists differed in that Goldstein believed a person could self-actualize at any moment, including the present and in different circumstances.[11] So, in some ways, self-directed learning can be thought of like self-actualization where the learner realizes their potential through learning that is both necessary and fulfilling. Figure 3.3 depicts this hierarchical structure.

Professional development is key to building and maintaining skills as a manager. Attending conferences, workshops, and training can be fun and insightful, but no matter how many of these activities you experience, there is much more that can be gained by personally directing your learning and facilitating your growth. Putting both the employer and employee perspective together concerning professional development can create a robust approach to development and growth. One way to focus on professional development is not to make assumptions about who is responsible for ensuring development and by approaching development with an open attitude about where and how to develop. Table 3.3 shows ten mistakes that some managers make when it comes to thinking about who is responsible for what, in their professional development.

Many of these "mistakes" highlight the fact that there is additional value in a self-directed approach. Formal professional development is valuable and useful for those interested in developing managerial proficiency, the onus is on you to experience, practice, and learn. As valuable as professional development can be, it can only take you so far on your development journey. Self-directed learning provides independence and a way to supplement the professional development opportunities you may get from employers or in formal education settings. Self-directed learning requires you to be resourceful and take initiative. It is a mindset that will serve you well no matter what organization, job, or transition you may face.

Table 3.3 Ten Mistakes About Professional Development

1. Assuming your employer is responsible for your development.
2. Assuming your organization will pay for the professional development you need.
3. Taking whatever professional development is offered regardless of how it fits in your professional development plan.
4. Not having a personal professional development plan.
5. Participating in professional development in body but not in spirit.
6. Going it alone – not engaging others in your professional development journey.
7. Going after only formal professional development; ignoring informal professional development opportunities that you create for yourself.
8. Assuming there should be a set time or amount of time designated for professional development.
9. Failing to practice what you've learned.
10. Ignoring the best resources for professional development – self.

Improving Self-directed Learning: Tips for Success

Self-directed learning allows people to continually invent and reinvent themselves by providing an avenue for learning and skill improvement. It is controlled by the learner and offers many options for management development, technical development, and personal development. Self-directed learning is a *way of being* when it comes to learning. It is an approach that is flexible, easily controlled, and effective. Self-directed learning differs from person to person and can be stopped or started as the learner deems appropriate.

Focus. Focus on being a self-directed learner every day. Embrace controlling your learning experience and follow a process for developing and executing a learning plan.

Maintain the right attitude. Have the self-confidence that you can accomplish your learning goals; have trust in yourself that your desire to learn is strong enough to fuel your learning initiatives. Make self-directed learning a mindset not something on your "to do" list.

Multiple perspectives. Get used to doing multiple things at once; for example, while you're in a meeting also focus on your learning agenda through observation. Look for opportunities to learn during regular work activities.

Start small. Try short and easy self-directed tasks; smaller successes will give you confidence to do more and bigger activities. Self-directed learning, as you will see in the descriptions of the tools later in the book, can be more involved so building your capacity to learn in a self-directed way will be important.

Identify resources that will help you. This can encompass websites, people, a special notebook or app, something that will aid in your learning journey. While self-directed learning does come from the "self" it does not say that accessing and using as many resources as are available, including other people, is not viable and important.

Develop habits and tactics to help. For example, consider creating a weekly self-directed learning "to do" list where you identify activities in your week (meetings, lunches, networking, conference calls, etc.) where you can apply self-directed learning.

Talk it up. Tell someone what you're doing; you don't need to disclose a lot of details if you prefer not to; however, you tell someone about your goal to build a competency, it becomes more real and you'll likely feel more accountable.

Don't be afraid to ask for help. If you're going to learn from doing, you'll need to have some help for things like role plays or to find resources and information. Self-directed means you're in control of the learning – not that you have to go it alone.

Reward yourself. Set up a reward system for yourself such that you give yourself something upon meeting a learning goal you've established. It can be dinner at your favorite restaurant, a weekend away, or anything you deem special. Reward yourself to keep up your motivation.

Measure results. Once you write down a goal and create a timeline you have something to measure. Either you accomplished the goal or you didn't and either you met the timeline or you didn't. If you didn't, try to figure out why so you can make adjustments as your learning journey continues.

Notes

1 Knowles, M. (1991). *The Adult Learner: A Neglected Species* (4th ed.). Houston: Gulf Publishing.
2 Gibbons, M. (2002). *The self-directed learning handbook: Challenging adolescent students to excel.* San Francisco, CA: Jossey-Bass
3 http://infed.org/mobi/self-directed-learning/
4 http://citeseerx.ist.psu.edu/viewdoc/download?doi=10.1.1.152.4176&rep=rep1&type=pdf
5 www.psychologytoday.com/us/articles/201607/the-golden-age-teaching-yourself-anything
6 Brookfield, S. D. (1995). Adult Learning: An Overview. In A. Tuinjman (Ed.), *International Encyclopedia of Education.* Oxford: Pergamon Press.
7 https://en.wikipedia.org/wiki/Eduard_C._Lindeman
8 www.bpastudies.org/bpastudies/article/view/38/78
9 http://ccnmtl.columbia.edu/projects/pl3p/Self-Directed%20Learning.pdf; https://en.wikipedia.org/wiki/Eduard_C._Lindeman; Knowles, M. (1991). *The Adult Learner: A Neglected Species* (4th ed.). Houston: Gulf Publishing.
10 https://positivepsychologyprogram.com/goal-setting-theory/
11 Whitehead, P. M. (2017). Goldstein's self-actualization: A biosemiotic view. *The Humanistic Psychologist*, Vol. 45, No. 1, 71–83.

Bibliography

Brookfield, S. D. (1985). Self-directed Learning: A Conceptual and Methodological Exploration. *Studies in the Education of Adults,* Vol. 17, No. 1, 19–32.
Brookfield, S. D. (1995). Adult Learning: An Overview. In A. Tuinjman (Ed.), *International Encyclopedia of Education.* Oxford: Pergamon Press.
Flora, C. (2016). The Golden Age of Teaching Yourself Anything. *Psychology Today.* July.

Gibbons, M. (2002). *The self-directed learning handbook: Challenging adolescent students to excel.* San Francisco, CA: Jossey-Bass.

Infed (Retrieved May, 2019). Self-directed Learning. Available: http://infed.org/mobi/self-directed-learning/

Hiemstra, R. (1994). Self-directed Learning. In T. Husen and T. N. Postlethwaite (Eds.), *The International Encyclopedia of Education* (2nd ed.). Oxford: Pergamon Press. Available: http://ccnmtl.columbia.edu/projects/pl3p/Self-Directed%20Learning.pdf

Houston, E. (2019). What is Goal Setting and How to do it Well. Available: https://positivepsychology.com/goal-setting/

Knowles, M. (1975) *Self-directed Learning: A Guide for Learners and Teachers.* New York: Cambridge Books.

Knowles, M. (1991). *The Adult Learner: A Neglected Species* (4th ed.). Houston: Gulf Publishing.

Manning, G. (2002). Self-directed Learning: A Key Component of Adult Learning Theory. *Business and Public Administration Studies*, Vol. 2, No. 2.

Whitehead, P. M. (2017). Goldstein's self-actualization: A biosemiotic view. *The Humanistic Psychologist*, Vol. 45, No. 1, 71–83.

Wikipedia (Retrieved July, 2019). Eduard C. Lindeman. Available: https://en.wikipedia.org/wiki/Eduard_C._Lindeman

4   Self-assessment

Any development process, self-directed or otherwise, needs to begin with an individual self-assessment. Conducting a self-assessment can give an individual a sense of where they are compared to where they'd like to be concerning personal skills and abilities. A self-assessment, to be effective, needs to consider an individual's work-related values, interests, personality type, and aptitudes. These personal characteristics make up who you are, and are typically considered when thinking about what to study in school or what career to pursue. In the context of this chapter, the discussion is about how to evaluate the competencies you need now and those to anticipate as your role and career evolve. Self-assessments provide a variety of benefits beyond straightforward skill assessment. They also offer an opportunity for self-reflection and may facilitate insights about career choice and direction.

A foundation of self-directed learning starts with self-awareness, and this can begin with a self-assessment. We know that self-directed learners are self-reliant, self-starting, and self-motivated. If we consider the "self" as an independent individual who has their own best interests in mind, then it makes sense to develop goals and learning objectives geared toward self and where, directionally, you see yourself from a developmental perspective. There are many different ways to accomplish a self-assessment; ranging from sitting down with a blank sheet of paper and identifying free hand your strengths and weaknesses, to taking formal self-assessments that are valid and based upon careful research. An assessment is a diagnostic tool that helps an individual, an instructor, or an organization, diagnose where they are on a learning journey, personality, or skill continuum. An assessment can measure current knowledge, health, mechanical performance, value, or other characterization. Some assessments are widely available for free on the Internet, and others are publicly available with fees associated with administration, scoring, and interpretation.

Formal Assessments

There are many assessments that both individuals and organizations can use to help describe and predict behavior. Some are popular and used by many organizations and coaches. For example, assessments like the Myers-Briggs Type Indicator (MBTI),[1] the Predictive Index (PI),[2] or Hogan Assessments[3] exist and are widely used. Although organizations sometimes sponsor the completion and interpretation of these assessments, they are also widely available to individuals either in full or partial form.[4] Even though these assessments are interesting and often quite informative, they are not specific for developing learning objectives or assessing particular competencies. Assessments such as these are commonly used to help facilitate career discussions or team dynamics discussions rather than learning goals. Some assessments are used by organizations in the talent management process to ensure they have competent candidates who may need less training than others.

An organization may want to use an assessment like the Predictive Index at the early stages of the recruitment process to ensure that a potential candidate is a good fit for the role to which they've applied. These types of assessments, and there are hundreds of them, which look at everything from specific skills to broad personality traits, are available online across the world to organizations and individuals who want to measure or appraise particular skills. Formal assessments such as these provide valuable information and may offer insights to individuals as to where they need to focus their learning efforts. For self-directed learning, though, informal assessments may offer a more fruitful source of awareness about what will be beneficial in developing your managerial proficiency.

Informal Assessment

A self-assessment carried out to identify learning opportunities is not a test, and as a result, individuals who conduct a self-assessment should feel comfortable in being as open and honest as possible in completing the assessment. This openness will result in maximum benefit because more accurate goals can be established. An informal self-assessment can be as simple as reflecting on how well or poorly you perform on a particular competency or task. As an example, someone may think about how well they did after a formal *presentation* to a group; they may even ask observers what they thought about the presentation. In its simplest form, this is a self-assessment. The self-assessment process can be a source of learning in and of itself. It is a process of self-reflection about your achievement and proficiency in specific skills. A self-assessment can also be more complex and delve deeper into skills, priorities, and other factors.

Competency Self-assessment

The competencies identified in Table 2.1 in Chapter 2 provide a starting point for assessing current managerial proficiency. For self-directed learning, there are two aspects of self-assessment to consider. First is your proficiency <u>level</u>, and the second is how <u>important</u> the competency is for you now and in the future. A proficiency self-assessment such as this indicates your view on how skilled you think you are on a particular competency. It is not a rating of what you know; it is a rating of how you perform in a given competency. The importance assessment indicates how essential you think being skilled in the competency is to your job and career now and at a future time.

Competency Proficiency Level

What makes a manager proficient? What makes one person more adept at one competency versus another? What accounts for someone being capable, but not consistent in demonstrating their skill? Proficiency is something that organizations typically strive for in their employees, and most of us strive for this in ourselves. That said, we may not have the same level of proficiency at a high level in all the competencies that we need, and we may not in practice require the same level of skill in all the competencies identified. Competence can be thought of as a level, and these levels can be depicted on a continuum from low to high. At the low-end, an individual may not be very skilled; they may be able to handle simple instructions but require close guidance. They may understand what needs to be done but not be able to execute it. At the upper end of the continuum, proficiency is quite high. It is characterized by superior performance that is consistent and for which others consider the individual an expert.

Using a simple scale to indicate how proficiently you demonstrate a behavior will be a gauge not only of your competence but also your confidence about the competency. Each competency has multiple components, so it is important to think about all aspects of the competency. You may do some aspects well but *not* others. When you complete the self-assessment exercise, respond based on your weakest area. Figure 4.1 indicates how the levels sit on the proficiency continuum. Starting on the left is where you might begin at your skill level. At the start of a career, most people will have little to no exposure to a particular skill. Over time, beginning as early as pre-university years, some competencies such as communication or ethics will start to be developed. As you gain experience, exposure, and classroom learning, your proficiency moves along the continuum. Keep in mind that if there is a gap in your experience and use of a competency then your skills may atrophy a bit and require development at multiple times in your career.

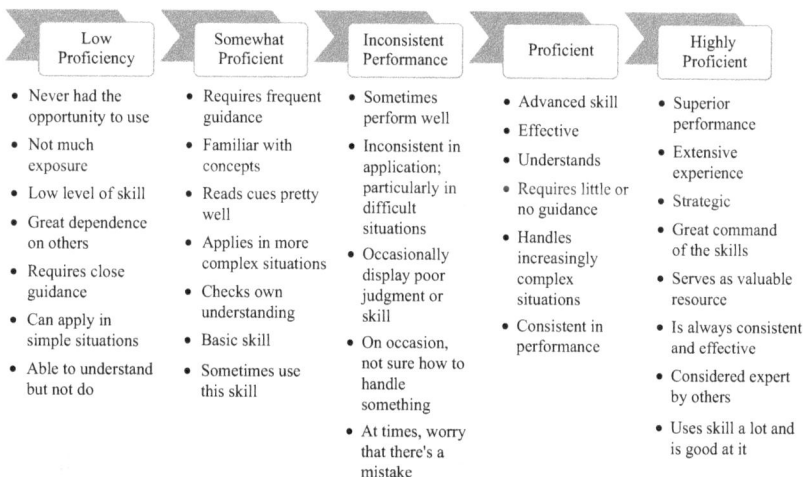

Low Proficiency	Somewhat Proficient	Inconsistent Performance	Proficient	Highly Proficient
• Never had the opportunity to use • Not much exposure • Low level of skill • Great dependence on others • Requires close guidance • Can apply in simple situations • Able to understand but not do	• Requires frequent guidance • Familiar with concepts • Reads cues pretty well • Applies in more complex situations • Checks own understanding • Basic skill • Sometimes use this skill	• Sometimes perform well • Inconsistent in application; particularly in difficult situations • Occasionally display poor judgment or skill • On occasion, not sure how to handle something • At times, worry that there's a mistake	• Advanced skill • Effective • Understands • Requires little or no guidance • Handles increasingly complex situations • Consistent in performance	• Superior performance • Extensive experience • Strategic • Great command of the skills • Serves as valuable resource • Is always consistent and effective • Considered expert by others • Uses skill a lot and is good at it

Figure 4.1 Competency Proficiency Level Continuum

Worksheet 4.1 provides an opportunity to begin your self-assessment. This self-assessment is for your personal use and does not need to be shared with anyone unless you choose to do so. Place a check mark or blacken one of the squares for each of the 50 competencies. Complete this exercise being as realistic as possible. If you rate yourself as Proficient or Highly Proficient in all 50 competencies you are likely not being realistic – we all have strengths <u>and</u> areas of opportunity. The outcome of this assessment will help guide you in your self-directed learning. It is a good idea to date this form and probably best to make a personal blank copy so that you can complete the assessment again in six or 12 months to assess your progress and to determine if your needs have shifted through job or assignment changes. On any competency, if you do one aspect well but struggle with another aspect, then in a self-assessment you should respond based on the aspect you do less well. For example, when rating *presentation skills*, if your presentation slides are clear and engaging, but your delivery is not that effective, then you should rate yourself overall as a "2" rather than a "4" for presentation skills. You may not need to develop the slide-side of your presentation skills, but you do not want to lose the need for improving the delivery-side of your presentation skills. A rating of "2" gets this competency on your priority list whereas a "4" may not.

If someone asks you what your strengths are or areas for improvement, you might be able to rattle off a few things rather quickly, especially on the strength-side. While you may be accurate on the general level, most of us can benefit from deeper introspection on where our behaviors fall on a proficiency level scale as well as importance scale. Upon completion of the first part of this self-assessment, you will have a sense of your strengths and weaknesses from a deeper and more useful perspective. Although informal, thinking about your behavior and proficiency on these competencies in a more structured way will help you to be more accurate. Some questions to ponder as you complete Worksheet 4.1 include:

- Am I uniform in my demonstration of this competency?
- Does my behavior depend on certain conditions such as how much sleep I've had or how many people are involved?
- Will my boss, peers, or subordinates all agree on my self-assessment? Why or why not?
- Have I had enough opportunity to exhibit behaviors for the competency to feel confident in my assessment? For example, if you're a new supervisor, you may not have had a chance to do much *delegating*.
- Do others look at me for guidance on this skill?
- Do I look to others for assistance in understanding and guiding my performance?
- Do I use the skill often or less often?

If I think my assessment on any given scale is different than what I think a boss, peer, or subordinate would think, then my assessment is probably not as accurate as it should be. If I score a goal the first time I play a sport, I may have had "beginner's luck" rather than demonstrating proficiency in the sport. The point is that many factors can influence our skill level at any time. The self-assessment is looking for how *consistently* you perform as this will provide a baseline.

Worksheet 4.1 Self-assessment: Management Competencies – Proficiency

Proficiency level: Rate your proficiency level for each competency using the following scale.
      5 – Highly proficient; considered by others as an expert
      4 – Proficient; advanced skill
      3 – Not much exposure/practice
      2 – Somewhat proficient; basic skill level
      1 – Not at all proficient; low level of skill

	5	4	3	2	1
Accountability:					
Adaptability:					
Analytical thinking:					
Building relationships:					
Building teams:					
Business acumen:					
Change management:					
Coaching:					
Collaboration:					
Communication:					
Conflict management:					
Continuous learning:					
Creativity:					
Customer orientation:					
Decision making:					
Delegating:					
Developing others:					
Diligence:					
Empowering others:					
Ethics:					
Finance and budgeting:					
Global mindset:					
Goal setting:					
Human capital management:					
Influencing others:					
Initiative:					

Worksheet 4.1 (Cont.)

	5	4	3	2	1
Innovation:					
Interpersonal skills:					
Leadership:					
Listening:					
Managing performance:					
Motivating:					
Negotiation skills:					
Networking:					
Organization:					
Organization awareness:					
Performance management:					
Planning:					
Presentation skills:					
Problem-solving:					
Project management:					
Results orientation:					
Risk-taking:					
Seeking/giving feedback:					
Strategic thinking:					
Stress management:					
Teamwork:					
Trust and respect:					
Valuing diversity:					
Work-life balance:					

Competency Importance

Getting a sense of your proficiency on each of the competencies is essential; however, the next critical question is, how important are each of the skills for your success now, and in the future? You can argue that each of the competencies is important to managers. While this is true, the context is whether or not the competency is essential to your job or career at present or in the next 12 months. Are there expectations that you take on *financial and budgeting* tasks? Will you be spearheading a change initiative? If the answer is "yes" to each of these questions, then you need to give a high rating of a "4" or "5" on an importance assessment. Keep in mind that everything can't be an immediate need and everything can't be highly important – all at the same time.

To complete the second part of the self-assessment, you will also need to think about how important this competency is to you <u>now</u>, and in the <u>future</u>. This information will help you to prioritize what you need to focus on in your learning plan. Realize that your assessment will be fluid about the importance of your skill development because your priorities are likely to shift based upon job assignments and roles you take on. Realistically, a learning plan can't focus on all 50 competencies. Narrowing your focus to a much smaller subset will allow you, as a learner, to set manageable goals. Thinking about the importance in terms of which competencies are important now and which will be called upon in the future, perhaps over the next 12 months, is one way to create meaningful parameters. This self-assessment is for your personal use and does not need to be shared with anyone unless you choose to do so. Complete this exercise being as realistic as possible. If all 50 items are Important or Highly Important, it will be difficult to prioritize which competencies to develop first. The outcome will help guide you in your self-directed learning.

One way to think about the importance of a competency is to think about how often you are called upon to use the skill. More importantly, perhaps, is how much value your supervisors, peers, and subordinates place on the competency. For example, *communication* is something that most people and organizations value and must do regularly. It is important, though, to think about this in the context of your role. Are you called upon to prepare formal communications? How much of your job involves communication that is essential to the performance of your work and the work of others? If your job is customer facing, it may be more critical for your success to be highly proficient at communication. Conversely, looking at a competency like creativity may yield a different rating if the use of creativity is infrequent or less relevant to your position. Importance, though, needs to also focus on the relevance of the competency for the future. If you know that your role will evolve or that there will be a new organizational initiative in the future, you may be able to anticipate that you will be called upon to be more creative or innovative in the future. If this is the case, importance may be a "2" now, but a "4" in the future. Some questions to ponder as you complete Worksheet 4.2 include:

- Why do you think this skill is critical now; have you been told this to be the case?
- Do you feel it is important to your current role? Does your job description say so?
- What is the relationship of the competency to your role? If it's listening, you likely do this all the time, but if it's making presentations, you may only do this sometimes.
- How essential is the competency in the next 12 months and beyond?
- Have you picked up feedback about the importance of this competency?
- How does the organization value this skill?
- Do others in the organization give this competency priority or view it as essential?

Worksheet 4.2 Self-assessment: Management Competencies – Importance

Importance: Rate the importance for each competency now and in 12 months from now using the following scale. Place a number in each box, in each of the two columns. Importance scale:

         5 – Highly important
         4 – Important
         3 – Not sure
         2 – Somewhat important
         1 – Not at all important

	Now	*In 12 Months*
Accountability:		
Adaptability:		
Analytical thinking:		
Building relationships:		
Building teams:		
Business acumen:		
Change management:		
Coaching:		
Collaboration:		
Communication:		
Conflict management:		
Continuous learning:		
Creativity:		
Customer orientation:		
Decision making:		
Delegating:		
Developing others:		
Diligence:		
Empowering others:		
Ethics:		
Finance and budgeting:		
Global mindset:		
Goal setting:		
Human capital management:		
Influencing others:		
Initiative:		
Innovation:		

Worksheet 4.2 (Cont.)

	Now	*In 12 Months*
Interpersonal skills:		
Leadership:		
Listening:		
Managing performance:		
Motivating:		
Negotiation skills:		
Networking:		
Organization:		
Organization awareness:		
Perceptivity:		
Performance management:		
Planning:		
Presentation skills:		
Problem-solving:		
Results orientation:		
Risk-taking:		
Seeking/giving feedback:		
Strategic thinking:		
Stress management:		
Teamwork:		
Trust and respect:		
Valuing diversity:		
Work-life balance:		

Completed proficiency level and importance worksheets may look something like those found in Example 4.1. This is a truncated list and demonstrates what you can learn by first assessing your skill level and second considering the importance of each. From this example, we can see that Nick needs to focus on both *building relationships* and *collaboration*. Not only are these very important in the future, he has rated his current proficiency level as relatively low compared to how important these skills are to him today. The next step is to build a plan.

Proficiency Development Plan

In creating a learning plan for developing management competencies, we know it is essential to, first, rate your proficiency level and the importance of each

Example 4.1 Nick's Self-assessment – Proficiency Level and Importance Ratings

Proficiency level: Rate your proficiency level for each competency using the following scale. 5 – Highly proficient; considered by others as an expert 4 – Proficient; advanced skill 3 – Not much exposure/practice 2 – Somewhat proficient; basic skill level 1 – Not at all proficient; low level of skill						Importance: Rate the importance for each competency now and in 12 months from now using the following scale. Place a number in each box, in each of the two columns. Importance scale: 5 – Highly important 4 – Important 3 – Not sure 2 – Somewhat important 1 – Not at all important		
	5	4	3	2	1		*Now*	*In 12 Months*
Accountability:		✓				**Accountability:**	2	3
Adaptability:			✓			**Adaptability:**	4	4
Analytical thinking:		✓				**Analytical thinking:**	2	3
Building relationships:				✓		**Building relationships:**	4	5
Building teams:					✓	**Building teams:**	1	3
Business acumen:		✓				**Business acumen:**	2	4
Change management:			✓			**Change management:**	3	4
Coaching:				✓		**Coaching:**	2	3
Collaboration:				✓		**Collaboration:**	3	5
Communication:		✓				**Communication:**	4	4

competency. Second, you must determine a timeline for when and how quickly you need improvement on each of the competencies you've identified. Keep in mind that as a "self-assessment," no one is going to verify your assessment – unless you ask them to do so, nor will a timeline be verified or enforced. It is, however, important that you have a plan, objectives, and a timeline to follow. Your purpose at this juncture is to consider each of the competencies independently and realistically think about how proficient you are and the importance of each. This combined assessment of proficiency level and proficiency importance will allow you to build a plan to set goals that are measurable and realistic.

Now that your assessment worksheets are completed it is time to hone in on a small number of competencies to begin your learning journey. Developing a learning plan for each to support your development needs comes next. At some point, you may need to focus on each competency listed in Table 2.1; however, trying to do all of them at once will minimize your effectiveness on any single proficiency. The Proficiency Development Plan highlighted in Worksheet 4.3 will help you to focus on a few key competencies together. It is possible to create multiple plans and to group various competencies. How many you choose is up to you. You

Worksheet 4.3 Proficiency Development Plan

	1st Priority	2nd Priority	3rd Priority	4th Priority
Competency				
Objective				
Time Frame				
Resources Needed				
Resources Available				
Self-directed Approaches				

Instructions: Use more than one worksheet if necessary. Another option is to create a single worksheet for each competency so that you have additional room for notes.

can copy the blank worksheet and have two or three worksheets – regardless of whether you initially focus on just a few of the competencies. Some may wish to initially focus on only a few of the competencies. Some may want to know all of the competencies on the learning journey up front and some may wish to repeat and review the assessment in six or 12 months to verify a need based on evolving responsibilities. The objective of this worksheet is to help you narrow your focus and to plan for what you need and how you will develop your proficiency.

Worksheet 4.3 lays out five factors to consider for each competency. Before considering these factors, take the competencies you've identified from the first part of the assessment and assign a priority. The worksheet accommodates four competencies, but you can start with fewer if you choose to do so. One way to approach this is to go through the proficiency level worksheet (Worksheet 4.1) and identify all the "1's" and "2's." Next, take this shortened list and consider the importance level (Worksheet 4.2) of "4's" and "5's." There is no equation to tell you how to prioritize, but this exercise will help you create some order or grouping of the competencies so that a learning plan can emerge. For each competency that you select as a priority, you will want to articulate an objective. Your overarching purpose, of course, is to improve your skill for the competency you identify and to include more specificity in a goal and time frame to make the intention clear and create a context for your learning. This will also help inform what self-directed learning tools to use and what resources you need. Finally, consider whether the importance is now, versus in the future. This will help you assign a proper time frame for development.

Consider the Following Example

If the competency you wish to develop as a #1 priority is *presentation skills*, this could have the following objectives:

- Prepare for a board presentation next quarter.
- Become more comfortable delivering presentations to be more effective.
- Improve delivery when giving presentations.
- Enhance the ability to put together a slide deck for presentation.
- Strengthen ability to read the audience during a presentation.

As you can see, these are quite different objectives, though all related to presentation skills. You may want to specify multiple objectives related to a single competency. See Example 4.2 for an illustration of what a completed Proficiency Development Plan may include for Chris, the senior manager who needs to develop her presentation skills. The development plan is for your use and should be used to guide your learning journey. It is best to assign a time frame for completion rather than leaving this aspect open. The more specific you are, the more likely you will be to work toward achieving the goal. The final factor on the Proficiency Development Plan involves deciding which self-directed learning opportunities will be the best fit for the development you need on the competency you've prioritized. It could be that just a few of the approaches are the ones that will facilitate learning the best or it could be that all five of the approaches highlighted in Chapters 5 to 9 will be appropriate. Learning more about the self-directed learning approaches in the following chapters will help you think through the best applications.

Improving Self-assessment: Tips for Success

A primary purpose of the self-assessment is to give yourself an anchor and a place to start. In reality, self-assessment is something that should be an ongoing process. Now that your assessment is complete, and you have identified your initial competencies to develop, the next step is to discuss self-directed learning tools

Example 4.2 Proficiency Development Plan – Chris

	1st Priority	*2nd Priority*	*3rd Priority*	*4th Priority*
Competency	Presentation skills	Goal setting	Empowering others	Collaboration
Objective	Improve presentation delivery skills in time for board presentation next quarter. • Learn to read audience • Enhance slide construction	Apply goal-setting tactics to assignments keeping myself and others on track	Improve my skill at empowering staff at all levels of performance and skill	Expand my approach to partner and exchange ideas with colleagues
Time Frame	0–3 months	3 months	3–6 months	6–9 months
Resources Needed	Draft of presentation deck to practice presentation	Examples of S.M.A.R.T goals	List of colleagues who are role models for empowerment	List of cross-functional teams across organization
Resources Available	• Internal data to complete deck draft • Colleagues to review content and delivery	• Several peers use goal setting for projects; ask for examples	• Talk with HR for tips about how to empower	• Scott, in Marketing, is well-known for his collaborative approach
Self-directed Approaches	• Observation • Role playing	• Questioning • Journaling	• Observation • Journaling	• Role playing • Networking

that will help you to improve your managerial proficiency. As you learn about these tools, you should find it easy to begin incorporating the concepts into your everyday routines and into your learning plan. Following a thoughtful process and conducting your self-assessment is going to result in a better assessment and a plan that is more likely to be pursued.

Be honest. For self-assessment to be effective in helping you to focus on your development needs, it is important to be open and straightforward in evaluating your skills so that you can articulate individual learning goals. It may feel uncomfortable to rate your skills on the low-end of the proficiency continuum, but the outcome of doing so will hopefully allow you to rate yourself higher the next time you do a self-assessment.

Conduct self-assessment often. Carrying out self-assessment regularly, both formally and informally, will provide guidance and direction for your continuous learning.

It will also help you get used to the idea of the proficiency levels and needs, which can shift over time depending upon use and need.

Engage others. Ultimately, it's up to you to do a self-assessment. However, engaging others in your conversation can provide insights you should consider. There's no need, unless you choose to do so, to tell someone that you are doing a self-assessment exercise. Asking how someone views your skill can be worked into informal conversations and can focus on one competency with one individual and another competency with another individual.

Test out your assessment. Once you've completed Worksheet 4.3, you now have a set of guiding objectives. If you're uncertain as to which competencies are the best priority, you can look at the list and prioritize by asking someone, either directly or indirectly, what they think. For instance, if you're comfortable with this approach, you can involve your supervisor in a discussion about what he or she thinks. If this is uncomfortable, then you can enlist the help of someone outside your immediate chain of command or workplace. A family member, friend, or colleague may be able to assist in discussing, either directly or indirectly, your plan. The key is that whomever you engage must have enough knowledge of you and your performance to be able to offer an opinion. Keep in mind though, at the end of the analysis, the decision of what to do must come from you.

Focus. Hone in on a few goals at a time and avoid taking on too many at once. Focus does not mean exclusivity – it is possible to develop multiple competencies at the same time while you are concentrating on just one or two. Focusing your attention on a few competencies allows your development to be concentrated rather than scattered.

Follow up with a learning plan. A self-assessment without a concrete learning plan will not likely result in behavior change. While awareness is essential, for self-directed learning to take place, there needs to be a learning plan with objectives and measurable goals. Putting this plan on paper creates accountability for the learner. The learner is the person in charge and articulating what you will do, how it will be accomplished and when, will allow for adjustments, if necessary, in future learning plans. That which is measured gets managed.[5]

Reassess. Periodically the learner must reassess their proficiency level on the given competency that they have identified as a priority. The goal, of course, is that proficiency will have increased. Besides, being able to move one goal off the learning plan, perhaps because it has been accomplished, will allow other priorities to be undertaken through self-directed learning.

Notes

1 www.mbtionline.com/
2 www.predictiveindex.com/
3 www.hoganassessments.com/

4 www.monster.com/career-advice/article/best-free-career-assessment-tools
5 http://extremelearners.com/what-gets-measured-gets-managed/

Bibliography

Conlan, C. (Retrieved July, 2019). 10 Awesome Free Career Self-assessment Tools on the Internet. Available: www.monster.com/career-advice/article/best-free-career-assessment-tools

Drucker, P. (1954, Retrieved July, 2019). What Gets Measured Gets Managed. Available: http://extremelearners.com/what-gets-measured-gets-managed/

Hogan (Retrieved July, 2019). The Science of Personality. Available: www.hoganassessments.com/

MBTI (Retrieved June, 2019). The Insightful You. Available: www.mbtionline.com/

Predictive Index (Retrieved July, 2019). The Talent Optimization Platform. Available: www.predictiveindex.com/

Part II

5 The Art of Networking

Networking is critically important to career success, whether you are trying to secure a job, learn, or expand your opportunities. The size of your network is often less important than the relevance of your contacts. The relevance of your existing network is sometimes less important than your ability to maneuver within and take advantage of this group of individuals. Your network is a treasure trove of knowledge and information and the *pathway* to more knowledge and information. Over and above your existing network, there are myriad ways to access new network opportunities. How you maneuver through your network, connect to the right people and draw out useful knowledge and information to develop your skills will be the difference between simply having a network and utilizing that network for developmental purposes.

You've probably been networking for years. You probably began networking before you ever realized what you were doing was called networking. When most people think of networking, their view is relatively traditional. Networking, the process of interacting for exchange, is a source of support, helps you with your current position, is a way to stay current on a topic area, and can be critical in a new job search. A self-directed learning view of networking adds many more components to the mix. When approaching networking from a self-directed learning point of view, you add the intention of learning something specific to the purpose of interacting for exchange. Networking provides an opportunity to observe specific behavioral competencies, a chance to practice individual competencies, and access to people who may know a lot about the skill you seek to develop. Table 5.1 compares a traditional view of networking to a self-directed learning view of networking.

Networking is more than business card swapping and connecting through social media platforms. To develop a lasting and valuable relationship, meeting over a drink or lunch may not be sufficient. Some people recoil from networking either because they are introverted, shy, or feel like a "fake" doing so. Researchers have found that there are two dominant motivational focuses when it comes to being open to learning through networking. In "promotional-focused" people, there is an open mind about the possibilities that networking can bring. For "prevention-focused" people, they see networking as a necessary evil and, as a result, engage in it less often. The outcome is that prevention-focused people tend to underperform

Table 5.1 Traditional Compared to Self-directed View of Networking

Traditional view of networking	Self-directed learning view of networking
• Can be either intentional or unintentional	• A mechanism for skill development
• Connecting with others is the goal	• A way to seek specific skill information
• Good source of support	• Can be targeted for a specific learning need
• Helpful during transitions	• Latitude to observe desired competency of others in action
• Helpful in performing job	
• Important for job search	• Learning formally
• Important to employing organization	• Learning informally
• More is better	• Opportunity to develop behavioral skills
• Opportunity to be productive in a non-office environment	• Opportunity to practice behavior competencies
• Time-consuming and sometimes awkward	• Planned and intentional
	• Treasure trove of useful knowledge
• Useful for career advancement	• Potentially time-consuming and can be viewed as a chore
• Not always enjoyed; seen as a chore	

in some aspects of their job. Further research has shown that it is possible to shift from a prevention to promotion mindset and begin to embrace "networking as an opportunity for discovery and learning rather than a chore."[1]

There is often a tendency to talk with the people we know, rather than those we don't know, when we are in social settings or at designated networking events. This can be valuable in that it helps to solidify and build a stronger relationship with colleagues we know. Interacting with those who we know can also be useful as well as being enjoyable. That said, this tendency is one that is safe and may, in the long run, not provide the needed access to people who can help you to build and develop your skills. Managers need to balance their everyday need for networking with using networking as a strategy for learning. For networking to be successful as a learning strategy, it needs to be *planned* and encompass more than a one-off event. This is not to say that you can't learn something at a single event or in a single encounter with someone you know or who has something valuable to contribute to your growth. While positive exchange occurs all the time, learning in practice will likely happen when there is more focus and more opportunity to experience the learning and aspects of learning by laying out a roadmap to do so. Before discussing a network learning strategy and plan, it is necessary to consider all the possible sources for learning through networking.

Sources for Networking

Taking into account that networking can occur just about anywhere at any time, there are many sources for networking that can be identified. Noting the potential sources allows people to build a plan for networking and to specifically look for varied opportunities. With a lens of networking for learning, objectives can be identified, and a network to develop specific competencies can be established. It is also likely that once you create a network to help with one competency, it may, at least in part, be very helpful in developing other competencies on your priority list. The following list shows how broad the possibilities are when thinking about where to network.

- Classmates or former classmates
- Coworkers including bosses and subordinates
- Family
- Former colleagues or coworkers
- Friends
- Friends of family members, friends, or colleagues
- LinkedIn, and other social media applications
- Neighbors
- On an airplane, train, or bus
- Professional organizations/gatherings
- Professors, teachers, or training instructors
- Social gatherings
- Volunteer organizations or affiliations

These sources can be broken down into networking *inside* your organization, *outside* your organization in professional settings, and among *family and friends*. A fourth source, the lucky accident,[2] can also be described, though this occurrence also fits with the outside your organization category.

Networking Inside Your Organization

Active internal networking can provide a robust range of benefits. Your internal network often helps you get your job done more efficiently or effectively and provides resources and information that can be useful for both career and personal reasons. Looking into your organization for support and learning can bring you closer to coworkers, bosses, and subordinates. In small organizations, you may know most of your coworkers; however, you may not interact with all of them regularly or as profoundly as the concept of networking may imply. Moreover, you may not know enough about them to fully appreciate how they can help you – or how you can support them. Sometimes in networking, the need to break down social barriers is as great, if not more so, than to break down physical or logistical barriers.[3] Internal social media platforms and intranets can assist in breaking down barriers – both socially and physically. Perhaps the best approach is to engage your coworkers *both* formally and informally when you're trying to learn something new. Asking a coworker what they're working on or if they know anything about X or Y competency can get a conversation started and can open a window into a more in-depth and focused discussion. More about how to do this in Chapter 7, The Art of Questioning.

From a learning perspective, worry less, or not at all, about the person's title or role. Focus on your learning objective and not about the position-side of your job or someone else's job. That is, try not to think about how much influence the other person has and whether or not you are worried they think you have an ulterior motive in trying to engage them through networking.[4] If you discover that a senior manager in another department or division of your organization is an expert in *project management* and this is one of your identified competency needs, then there should be nothing wrong with approaching this individual to build a stronger relationship for learning. If you met this person at the coffee shop in the lobby of your building for the first time and by chance learned of their expertise, you may have genuinely and honestly asked questions and for advice. The fact that they have influence in your organization should not change your need – but may influence your approach. Depending upon how political your organization is or what your boss is like, you may want to let him or her know that you'll be reaching out to network with another senior manager and you may also want to tell the senior manager about your learning objective. Be clear and genuine, and you will likely find people to be happy to help. These cautions are valid in both small and large organizations.

The bottom line is that there is a potential wealth of knowledge inside your organization, some of which will be easy to identify, and some of which may be hidden from your immediate view. Taking the time to explore what may offer easy access and prove useful, can provide a significant return. A final internal source, which is a bridge to the external, is our friends, colleagues, and other people inside your organization who your network may know. The more proactive you are in pursuing connections and building relationships, the more successful you're likely to be. One way to approach this is by asking coworkers (family and friends too) if they have any good sources to recommend to you and if they are willing to facilitate making a connection. Getting a name and contact information is helpful; having a personal introduction is typically much more effective. Just as you may not know all of the skills and abilities of a coworker, boss, or subordinate, you may not know about a useful source that your personal connections may have. Even if you find good sources inside your organization for the competency you seek to develop, it is always helpful to have multiple sources for learning. When you are on a learning journey, always try to be proactively looking for connections that can help.

Networking Outside Your Organization

External networking provides the deepest and broadest pool for sources of learning. There are formal networking sources such as professional meetings, conferences, and training events which often have built-in networking opportunities where attendees are encouraged to interact. An advantage of this type of source is that people may feel more comfortable engaging with someone they do not know since the underlying purpose is relationship building. A challenge here is to avoid networking with people you already know. Take the initiative to be promotion-focused in settings such as these. In a sense, you have built-in permission to do networking and should feel less awkward about it. If you are attending a formal course that is focused on developing either your technical or managerial competency, it may be tempting to think that you and the other participants are in the same position in terms of needing to learn something. While this may be true, it is also possible that someone in this setting may know of a resource or a person that could be helpful to you in your learning journey. They may even be able to help you directly with what they know how to do, and you them.

Other less formal, though excellent sources of external networking include former classmates, coworkers, bosses, and subordinates, as well as professors and instructors. In recent decades and with social media platforms such as LinkedIn, Twitter, and Facebook, it has become much easier to find and stay in touch with people whom you've worked with or met along your career and education road. Keeping up with your network is as essential as it is to continue to build your network. Engaging your network or trying to make one when you need it is not going to be as effective, *or as fast*, as when you have continuously kept up with your network, so it is available when you need it. We know this to be true for when you're looking for work and the same is certainly true when your purpose is learning.

Volunteer organizations, including religious and personal affiliations, can also provide valuable connections to assist with learning. While some volunteer work is associated with your professional focus, much of it relates to things that we value personally and passionately. Whether it is a social, health, humanitarian, or another issue, when volunteering, you are often put together with people who you may never have come across through your job or profession. Seeing *self-confidence, customer orientation, multitasking, trust*, and other behavioral competencies in action from people in different occupations, ages, social statuses, and other diverse aspects can be very insightful and informative. While a desire to further your career could drive your impetus for volunteering to do something, often the purpose is more personal or altruistic. That said, there is no reason not to capitalize on what is in front of you. The people you come in contact with externally will likely respond positively when you attempt to engage them for learning. Be clear about your purpose and intention.

Friends and Family

People who are close to you personally are also potential sources of networking. Family and extended family, like volunteer organizations, offer access to people who are in many different professions and who have different skills and backgrounds. These people connect to many others with whom they work and interact. While you interact with family, the topics may cover kids, family events, shared history, and the like. It is not unusual to talk about jobs, education, and other professionally-related areas. A neighbor may be someone you only see occasionally, or with whom you talk about the yard and other local events, but here, again, is a potential opportunity for learning. While networking in your organization or externally may make you feel awkward asking for assistance, family and friends should offer a more comfortable avenue to some. Regardless of how close you are to a family member or friend, it is still important to be professional and to be clear about the assistance you seek. Always follow up and always be respectful of the people to whom you connect.

Creating a Networking Plan

There are multiple ways to approach building a learning plan for networking. First, there is the informal plan where you have a competency in mind, and you begin to explore more about the skill in terms of what best practices look like, where you may find more information, and who can potentially assist. As you move through your routine of work and activities, including networking, you may begin to gather information and ideas about how to tackle the new learning objective you've established. An advantage of this informal approach is that you can have a few competencies in mind as you explore possibilities. As you do this, it will be imperative that you capture the ideas and names of people with whom to follow up. Keeping a journal is an excellent way to approach this – more about the art of journaling in Chapter 9.

A more formal way to approach networking with a learning purpose is to build a plan around a single competency and think about all the people and aspects you will need to explore so that you have a more robust learning plan. It is certainly possible to pursue multiple competencies at once from a networking perspective, but you will want to complete separate plans for each. As can be seen in Worksheet 5.1, you will want to think about the relevant people you may know for further brainstorming about possible connections, as well as the appropriate sources for meeting new people who may be able to assist. As a result, this plan becomes a working document that may take a little time to complete. You can begin compiling the information you need during informal networking, or in advance of more formal networking. In addition to identifying relevant people and sources, you will also want to begin thinking about the questions you want to answer in pursuit of your competency development as well as the resources you want to uncover. For example, in addition to identifying other people and content, you may want to determine if there are any relevant training courses, books, articles, websites, and additional applicable information. You may or may not take a class or buy a book, but at this juncture, you are collecting as much as you can. As you talk with more people about the competency and best practices, you can begin to filter what resonates with you and what is within the realm of possibilities for you to accomplish. Another part of the plan is to think about any budget or financial considerations that may exist as well as who, if anyone, you need to inform or consult. Some networking comes with a cost – either financial, time, or both. It is easy to be drawn in by a new idea or excitement about developing a new competency but it is also essential to think about the resources you will need to expend.

Once you have completed the top portion of the worksheet and have thought about what time or money you need to invest, you should build a plan for a specified period of time. The worksheet suggests eight weeks, but you have the latitude in deciding what makes the most sense given your priorities, time, and budget. There may be weekly opportunities for events, or there could be monthly or quarterly events. With things you schedule for yourself, it may be that it takes you several weeks to schedule a networking lunch, and this could be for a date much further in the future. The point is that you begin to plan and focus on a

Worksheet 5.1 Networking Plan

Competency:		Date:
Objective:		

Brainstorming: relevant events, potential people, questions, and resources

Relevant sources for networking:	Relevant people for networking:
1.	1.
2.	2.
3.	3.
4.	4.
5.	5.
Questions to ask during networking:	Resources to seek during networking:
1.	1.
2.	2.
3.	3.

Who, if anyone, to inform or consult about plan:

Budget or financial considerations:

Plan: strategy for events and people to engage and in what order; build 8 to 12-week plan

Week one:	Week two:
Week three:	Week four:
Week five:	Week six:
Week seven:	Week eight:

competency. Approaching networking with a goal-setting point of view will allow you to accomplish more and be more effective in your self-directed learning plan. Research on goal setting shows that when you create specific and measurable parameters that are realistic and achievable, you will accomplish more than if you simply promise yourself "to do the best" that you can.[5]

In addition to an overall plan for networking, for some of the encounters you have, it will be essential to have a well-developed outline or blueprint of what you want to accomplish. We've all heard someone say, "I'd like to pick your brain about something." Often the people on the receiving end of this are happy to oblige and may even be flattered. Many times, you get what you need, a piece of information or lead on where to get the information you need. If what you're looking for isn't a single piece of information but rather a desire to build a particular competency, then approaching the learning and a specific person with a more detailed plan can add far greater effectiveness. For example, if you know that your role or your organization is going to require you to have more of a *global mindset* or familiarity with a particular culture other than your own, you can develop a plan that involves individual and self-guided learning as well as learning through others who may have the knowledge, skills, and abilities to help or who can introduce you to others who can help. Worksheet 5.1 provides one approach to a learning plan that may be useful.

The more specific you can be in your planning the more likely you are to develop your skill on any given competency. Recall Dara, the middle manager described in Chapter 2. One of the future needs she has identified is to develop a *global mindset* to help position herself for promotion and other roles in the future. Dara can easily build a learning plan to meet this need. She is not under any immediate time pressure, so creating a thoughtful plan that allows her to explore a lot of options is quite realistic. Example 5.1 provides an example of what Dara's networking plan may include. Notice that because Dara is under no immediate time pressure to develop this skill, she has given herself a full three months to focus on developing this competency.

Another important aspect of networking is planning for a more formal networking meeting or exchange. It can range from a casual conversation of "picking someone's brain" to a more prescribed conversation in which you have very specific objectives you want to accomplish. Worksheet 5.2 lays out the blueprint for a networking meeting. This could be a meeting over a meal, coffee, drink, or even a plan to meet at a professional gathering or conference. Thinking through the context will be necessary because the context could influence the dynamics and what you will be able to accomplish. If what you are seeking from an individual is to get names and ideas, that's one thing, but if what you're trying to get is more in-depth information or a more substantive dialogue, that is another. Plan ahead to ensure that the interaction will accomplish what you want. Be mindful that you are not presumptuous about time or location and that you acknowledge that your request must fit in with the receiver's schedule and workload pressures. Someone who is an "expert" is likely to be busy.[6] It is always a good idea to follow up with someone after a meeting to thank them for their time and insights. Example 5.2 shows an illustration of the preparation that Dara may do for a one-on-one networking meeting.

Networking is a robust activity that offers enrichment and opportunities. It can be helpful with just about any competency or skill you wish to develop and is far more effective if you plan the activity as Dara has done for developing a *global mindset*. A point to keep in mind is that most of the principles discussed in this

Example 5.1 Networking Plan – Dara

Competency: *Global mindset*	Date: 08/22/2020

Objective: *Understand the global side of our business and develop an awareness of different cultures and how to work cross-culturally.*

Brainstorming: relevant events, potential people, questions, and resources

Relevant **sources** for networking:	Relevant **people** for networking:
1. *Local Women in Technology (WIT) chapter*	1. *My boss*
2. *Global sales department in organization*	2. *Steve W. in Global Sales department*
3. *Course on cross-cultural awareness*	3. *Astrid, member of Women in Technology*
4. *Local professional gatherings*	4. *Wilton, husband of my cousin who is from outside the country*
5. *My son's Scout meetings*	5. *Shannon, friend who has traveled extensively*
Questions to ask during networking:	**Resources** to seek during networking:
1. *How do you develop a global mindset? How do you know when you have one?* 2. *What are the behaviors of someone with a global mindset? What behaviors do they avoid?* 3. *Are there ways to practice?*	1. *Courses, books, articles to read* 2. *Identify people from other cultures to get to know* 3. *Partners with whom to conduct role plays*

Who, if anyone, to **inform or consult** about plan: *Need to tell Steve (boss) and need to let husband know that this may take some extra time and perhaps money.*

Budget or financial considerations: *Already paying WIT dues; may need to buy some lunches or coffee and may want to take a course – hopefully company will pay the fee.*

Plan: strategy for events and people to engage and in what order; build 8 to 12-week plan

Week One: *Begin general research to be prepared for networking.*	**Week Two**: *Read research and continue to look for relevant sources.*
Week Three: *Reach out to existing network for assistance and more connections from them.*	**Week Four**: *Begin approaching people to set up further discussions. Look internally.*
Weeks Five–Eight: *Begin to schedule external opportunities; set up a list of priorities.*	**Weeks Eight–Ten**: *Set up at least 1–2 meetings a week an d register to attend networking activities.*
Weeks 10–12: *Continue meeting with internal and external resources.*	**Weeks 10–13**: *Begin planning to do other activities such as role play, observation, and practice.*

Worksheet 5.2 Networking Meeting Preparation

Competency:	Date:
Objective: *write a statement about the competency you wish to develop. Be as specific as possible.*	
Who: *list the person with whom you will network*	**When**: *date of the networking meeting/event*
Referral: *who, if anyone, helped with this connection*	**Questions**: *plan when you will prepare your questions for the meeting*
Context/where: *identify the context; professional gathering? One-on-one? Lunch? Others present? In-person or virtual? Time zone difference?*	
What: *what are the questions you will ask; what resources or other connections will you seek?*	
Advance planning: *what do you need to read and how do you need to prepare so that your session will be as effective as possible?*	
Follow-up: *Can you suggest anyone? May I use your name? Are there any resources you'd suggest? Would you mind making an introduction?*	

chapter also apply to anyone, whether or not you are currently working inside an organization. For those in transition, just finishing a formal education program, or returning to the workplace after an absence, the concepts included are relevant and should be helpful to keep you organized and moving in the right direction. While in transition, your focus may be on finding your next opportunity, but it can also include a need to develop your skills and behaviors to be prepared for your next opportunity.

Improving Networking Effectiveness: Tips for Success

If we describe networking as the exchange of information and ideas, then is it different from learning? After all, learning is the acquisition of knowledge. To

Example 5.2 Networking Meeting Preparation – Dara

Competency: *Global mindset*	**Date**: *10/12/2020*
Objective: *Meet with someone who is an expatriate or from another country to learn about their experiences as an expatriate and as someone who has a cross-cultural and virtual team to learn about her background and experience.*	
Who: *Astrid, president of local WIT chapter*	**When**: *10/15/2020*
Referral: *Sheri, senior IT person in my organization who knows Astrid personally and helped me secure a lunch meeting with her.*	**Questions**: *Prepare list the Friday before; review and revise over the weekend.*
Context/where: *Danny's Pub, a restaurant located near Astrid's office. Astrid will have been traveling the previous week to Australia for work and has another trip planned to Eastern Europe at the beginning of next month.*	
What: • *How did you get started in IT?* • *When did you do your first expatriate assignment and in how many countries have you lived?* • *What do you see as some of the more prominent cross-cultural issues?* • *How did you develop your global mindset?* • *What are some of the experiences that stick out in your mind?* • *What would you suggest to someone like me who is interested in becoming more cross-culturally aware and who wants to advance in a global company?*	
Advance planning: • *Block out at least 2 hours on calendar to account for travel and a relaxed lunch.* • *Meet with Sheri to find out what she knows about Astrid.* • *Review some of the research from a few weeks ago to be familiar with the topics we may discuss.* • *Look up something about Australia and then test out your interpretation with someone who has recently traveled there.*	
Follow-up: *Can you suggest anyone? May I use your name? Would you mind making an introduction?* *Are there any resources you'd suggest?* *Are there any classes that you think would be helpful?*	

develop specific competencies, the addition of knowledge must be structured and funneled toward a particular goal. Acquiring new knowledge to develop a competency, like baking a cake or building a race car, takes the right ingredients in the correct amounts to assemble a credible finished product. Without the carburetor or eggs, the outcome will not be useful. Thus, networking in a self-directed context takes on a more robust definition and encompasses more components. The onus, however, is squarely in the learner's camp to drive the learning, structure the exchange, and create the desired outcome. Although the target of your efforts may be a willing participant, they may or may not be fully aware of your agenda. Your learning is not dependent upon the target being an official instructor.

Bring the right attitude. Your mindset and planning are essential. Approaching networking with a positive attitude and one that embraces learning is imperative. The people with whom you interact will quickly pick up on a negative or less than genuine posture. Showing excitement for learning can be infectious.

Be prepared at all times. Keep a list of questions and/or objectives with you at all times and review them regularly. You never know when you may have a "lucky accident" and meet someone who can help you with your behavioral learning objectives. Have a brief pitch of your learning objective and be clear about what you want to ask and how you want to follow up for further networking.

Ask questions and probe. Take advantage of what's in front of you and seek new knowledge. Try not to feel rushed in your discussion. Probe for additional expertise and resources. Be like a sponge and soak up all that the networking opportunity has to offer – including a request for further interaction.

Write it down. If you learn something useful or obtain a new lead, write it down as soon as possible or send yourself a note; use a smartphone or a physical notebook, whatever works best. Often in an open networking event, you will be meeting many people, and it may be challenging to keep track of all the names and information. Capture as much as you can while it is fresh in your mind.

Reciprocate. Networking is especially useful when both parties benefit. Be a sponge and also be a fountain. Pay it forward. You may have behaviors that someone else can emulate, and you may have resources that will be helpful to someone else. Even if there is no reciprocation at that moment, it may come back to you positively at a later time. This will help you build a positive reputation as someone who supports and should be supported.

Be appreciative. Never take for granted someone's insight, or assistance or time. Both in the moment and as a follow-up, show your gratitude for not only the content and connections you receive but also for the time the person has given you.

Keep expanding your network. The time to network is not just when you need something but *always*. The better your network, the better it will be when you need it. It takes time and effort to build a network – it is like a garden which takes care, feeding, weeding, and planting.

Connect the dots. Ensure that you know what knowledge, skills, and abilities someone has when you meet them. A business card does not usually tell you enough about a person. Learn more about them as a professional and as a person – go beyond their title or the company for whom they work. Building a relationship allows you to connect the dots.

Be genuine. Don't act contrary to who you are – many people can tell when someone is authentic versus forced. This sincerity is likely to get you more time and openness from someone who has the expertise to offer and who may often be asked to share their knowledge.

Epilogue. Always follow up either with a note or a social media connection; don't just invite someone to connect, always personalize the invitation. Even if you are appreciative in person with someone, following up with a personalized note will help to solidify the relationship.

Notes

1 https://hbr.org/2016/05/learn-to-love-networking
2 www.networkwise.com/tag/networking-tips/; www.sciencemag.org/careers/2002/05/networking-how-get-good-connection
3 https://theconversation.com/research-shows-networking-is-painful-but-it-can-be-a-lot-better-96854
4 www.forbes.com/sites/glennllopis/2012/05/29/7-reasons-networking-can-be-a-professional-development-boot-camp/#775d16316e90
5 https://iedunote.com/goal-setting-theory
6 www.nytimes.com/2019/03/17/smarter-living/the-right-way-to-ask-can-i-pick-your-brain.html

Bibliography

Bomzer, D. (2002). Networking: How to Get a Good Connection. *Science Magazine.* Available: www.sciencemag.org/careers/2002/05/networking-how-get-good-connection

Casciaro, T., Gino, F., and Kouchaki, M. (2016). Learn to Love Networking. *Harvard Business Review.* Available: https://hbr.org/2016/05/learn-to-love-networking

EduNote (Retrieved July, 2019). Goal Setting Theory of Motivation. Available: https://iedunote.com/goal-setting-theory

Goldfarb, A. (2019). The Right Way to Ask, 'Can I Pick Your Brain?' Available: www.nytimes.com/2019/03/17/smarter-living/the-right-way-to-ask-can-i-pick-your-brain.html

Llopis, G. (2012). 7 Reasons Networking Can Be a Professional Development Boot Camp. *Forbes.* Available: www.forbes.com/sites/glennllopis/2012/05/29/7-reasons-networking-can-be-a-professional-development-boot-camp/#a733ca6e900b

Rabus, C. (2019). Networking Tips. *Networkwise.* Available: www.networkwise.com/tag/networking-tips/

Sander, L. (2018). Research Shows Networking Is Painful, but It Can Be a Lot Better. *The Conversation.* Available: https://theconversation.com/research-shows-networking-is-painful-but-it-can-be-a-lot-better-96854

6   The Art of Role Playing

The purpose of role playing is to allow a person to practice a skill or ability they wish to develop. Applying what you learn in a simulated situation allows you to be more effective and comfortable in a real situation. With role play, a learner can practice several things simultaneously, can get real-time feedback, and can adjust their behavior almost immediately. Role play is flexible in that it may or may not include other players depending upon the learner's preference, time, or resource availability. In addition to behavioral learning, role play can be cognitively beneficial in understanding concepts and content. A key feature of role play is that the learner places themselves in the shoes they wish to fill or in another person's shoes altogether. In other words, they are "acting" as they wish to behave. Role play builds on a person's knowledge and experience by compelling them to think through how they will behave in a given situation. It enables the learner to experience the situation, or create a situation, to prepare for a future interaction. Role play is valuable because it allows for practice in a safe and nonthreatening way.[1]

Role play has been an accepted learning tool for a very long time. It is often used in school settings and in training programs. A key reason is that role play facilitates retention of learning.[2] One of the strengths of role play is that it allows the learner to make abstract problems or interactions into more concrete scenarios.[3] Another strength is that it can provide immediate feedback. If a learner is role playing with another person, not as a solo actor, they can experience a genuine reaction to something they say or do. This allows for the opportunity to speculate on attitudes, feelings, and uncertainties that may be present in the future situation. Replicating a role play may also allow for comparisons of approaches and responses. Role play involves applying knowledge, skills, and abilities to a situational problem. The learner needs to be integrative in applying what they know, what they've experienced, and how they respond in real time. Role playing decreases the gap between thinking and doing. The sales associate who is taught about customer service goes through a lot of training for greeting and responding to customers in a variety of scenarios. Over time, the responses become more routine for the different customer interactions they face.

Benefits of Role Play

Role playing as a method for learning has many benefits. First, and perhaps most importantly, it allows learners to be able to practice a skill or set of behaviors in a safe environment. Role playing calls for the learner to step outside his/her customary role, or, to give up their usual pattern of behavior. One way for a learner to learn from role play is through open discussion of the behaviors they display, and/or their reactions to the behaviors of others. Role play by its nature is somewhat unstructured, there is no script. Table 6.1 shows the benefits of role playing. In networking, a person is trying to learn about a competency and to connect with others to learn from their expertise and watch their behaviors. In role playing, you are trying the behaviors out for yourself. Role play is a hands-on, creative, low-cost, and practical way to build managerial skills and develop norms, in confidence – much like the sales associate who learns routines for greetings and responses. A difference is that with managerial competencies the range of behavioral skills needed is much broader.

A primary objective of role play is for you to retain the knowledge and behaviors you need. Key to this is changing or influencing the learner's perspective, increasing their empathy, and then facilitating greater engagement. Role play, due to its experiential nature, should lead to greater retention of learning and the behaviors that are sought to increase managerial proficiency. In addition, a role play is likely to increase your motivation to be successful in "real" situations. And if the scenario is one with multiple complexities, the role play is likely to lead to greater understanding and insight.

Role play may not work well for all situations; but it's ideal for some. A more formal role play takes time to develop and organize; particularly if there is a need to enlist the help of partners who will need to prepare and who are asked to provide honest feedback. Using a role play with partners can work well with fellow managers who also need to practice in preparation for similar interactions. Interviewing candidates, performance appraisal discussions, and presenting to senior management are a few that come to mind. Many of these scenarios have complexities and uncertainty concerning the reactions you will get. The idea

Table 6.1 Benefits of Role Playing

• Anticipate questions or issues from others	• Gain alternative perspectives
• Be actively engaged in learning	• Improve interpersonal skills
• Be creative	• Learn control
• Build confidence	• Learn in a safe environment
• Build desired habits	• Low-cost
• Build empathy	• Practical
• Build communication skills	• Practice by repetition
• Develop listening skills	• Repeat the scenario discussion multiple times for better practice
• Develop problem-solving options	• See concrete examples
• Facilitate attitude changes	• See the whole situation

of practice can help the learner ease their stress, develop empathy, and enhance their proficiency. There is often ample lead time before these preplanned events to organize role play interventions. Even with advanced planning and individual preparation, both the learner and the partner can be uncomfortable and emotions can run high if the issue is sensitive. As a result, although the benefits are many, there are drawbacks and this must be managed. It is possible that the learners will not get the feedback they need or want if these factors are not taken into consideration. Another drawback of role play when done with a partner is that it may be indicative of the players' current skill level and not be at a level to which you strive.[4]

Role Play in Action

Role play is a very flexible learning tool. It can take several forms, can be done in a very planned way, or can be a spur of the moment activity. Role play can help managers on a day-to-day basis and can also be helpful in developing managerial proficiency in most, if not all, of the competencies identified in Chapter 2. Some of the competencies are easy to visualize as role plays; delegating, influencing others, negotiating skills, listening, and so forth. Others, such as prioritizing or accountability, may be less likely to jump out as skills that can benefit from role play. However, there are ways that these behaviors may be practiced effectively. Consider accountability; where a person accepts responsibility for tasks, assignments, and timelines for completion and results. A manager may need to build this skill by developing behaviors and habits that demonstrate their accountability. Additionally, they may need to practice communicating their intent for being accountable with others. This could include the language used, the delivery, and may include some questions to convey that they want all of the important details on how to follow through on the tasks and complete an assignment to the satisfaction of the assignor. A role play can get a learner in a mode where they are careful to define what is expected and thoughtful in restating how they can be accountable.

Role Playing on Your Own

People often think of role play as something that must be done with at least one partner. However, this is not at all the case. A modified role play can easily be done by yourself and can be effective in practicing behaviors and discussions about behavior. In your head, have you ever practiced what you will say to someone? Chances are, you've done this many times in the past. Greeting someone important, giving a speech, reacting to something you expect someone to say, and so forth are examples of things we all want to get right and be effective at so we likely try to practice what we will say. While you might do this in your head, you've probably also done this out loud in the privacy of your car, shower, kitchen, or office. Doing this type of exercise can be helpful in not only practicing but also in building confidence. When trying to develop behaviors like leadership, integrity, influencing others, coaching, empowering others, and so many more, rehearsing what you want to say so that you say it effectively is very important. There are many places and times when you can find the privacy you need to conduct these types of role plays. Self-directed and individual role play practice can build skills from the simple to the more complex.

Worksheet 6.1 provides some examples of relatively simple scenarios that a manager may encounter. To help you get into the habit of role playing and to see how it can work for you to role play on your own, try out some of the scenarios. Get in character for the scenarios. To do so, try to think of a specific employee or someone you know. Talk out your role and imagine the response you might get from the person you're thinking about for the scenario. React and examine how you feel and why you feel it. You can practice this in the mirror, the shower, your car, in your office (with the door shut), or sitting on a park bench, where it may be best to do this in your head rather than out loud! In addition to these scenarios, try making a list on your own at the start of the week for discussions or issues that you know may be coming up. The more you practice, the more role play on your own becomes a tool that you can use on a regular basis to help you develop your skills and hone your behaviors.

Role Play with a Partner

Traditional role play occurs when at least two people take on roles and engage in a practice dialogue. These role plays can be either planned in advance or spontaneous. Planned role play can range from the informal to the formal. For example, if you know that your boss wants to discuss a project with you, you may ask a friend or spouse to help you prepare over coffee. You may want to do this if, for example, you think the discussion is about why the project is over budget or late. Practice can help you be clearer in your responses. On the formal side, if you have something that is more involved and requires a strong command of details you may want to arrange for a longer time, a more formal setting such as an office or a conference room, and bring in actual reports, data, and other specifics that are likely to be used when the real scenario plays out. Pitching a new product to a client, for example, can be practiced using other employees as stand-ins for the client. In a more formal role play scenario like this, it will be more effective if role play partners are given assigned roles and instructions for playing their parts.[5] For example, ask one employee to purposefully play the role of a naysayer, one who questions the data, one who focuses on the cost, and so forth. Thinking through the potential issues in a situation and assigning these roles can make the practice role play much more effective in preparing for the actual sales pitch.

The Role of Feedback

Any role play can be helpful in terms of practice; however, if your objective is to gain proficiency and skill then you need to be sure that you are practicing the correct behaviors or changing ineffective behaviors. For this to occur you need to work with role play partners who are willing to provide honest and helpful feedback. Moreover, the partners need to have the skills or understanding themselves for what they are trying to help you learn. This will involve getting reactions that

Worksheet 6.1 Role Playing on Your Own

Instructions:

- *Find a quiet spot where you will be comfortable practicing a role play*
- *Get into character for one of the scenarios below*
- *Prepare some notes around what you want to accomplish*
- *Practice the role play scenario multiple times and adjust the conversation until you are comfortable with the interaction*

Common scenarios:

1. A phone call where you are asked to go to a meeting in 45 minutes that's not on your schedule and for which you don't have time

2. A poor performer

3. A timid subordinate assigning a task

4. Talking to your boss's boss

5. Talking to a high performer about a task

6. Unengaged employee

7. You go to the copy machine and it's out of paper (again) or it's jammed (again); talking to a peer, your staff associate, or anyone else about the situation

8. You witness a peer call out his or her subordinate in a negative way and in front of others

9. You're talking to a peer about an upcoming meeting where there may be conflict

10. You're asked to defend your budget proposal unexpectedly

Create your own scenarios:

1.

2.

3.

4.

5.

6.

7.

8.

9.

10.

---

include constructive criticism, helpful suggestions, and observations that you may not be able to do on your own. As a result, your role play partner or participants need to be able to clearly articulate what they see as either effective or ineffective. In some cases, this may mean that they need to be a subject matter expert and, in other cases, just be able to interpret behaviors. Conducting a role play for a sales pitch with subordinates who are not willing to tell you that you haven't been clear in your communication or are not being influential in your delivery, will not provide learning or proficiency development. The right role play partners are needed if good feedback and skill development is to occur.

Case Studies

Role play activities are effective for situations that you anticipate and for which you want practice. A related activity is that of the case study. The case study is a common teaching method in both education and training. A case study can offer learning opportunities from things that have happened in the past. A case study can include a role play but more often includes a discussion of what happened along with what should happen next or how a problem can be solved. An advantage of a case study analysis is that it can result in greater understanding of complex situations. Doing a case study, followed by role play, can result in better retention of the learning materials and increased understanding as to the "why" behind an interaction or response. A case study may also provide an opportunity to gather the opinions of others – which can contribute to the development of your own opinion or interpretations. For example, a case study about a product failure can provide insights into risk-taking, finance and budget, global marketing, or results orientation. These insights can help a learner plan for a more effective role play.

How Role Play Works

Role plays conducted on your own can be helpful in practicing delivery and thinking through different possible reactions and behaviors. Role play on your own may lack feedback from a partner but can still provide information and response practice. If a manager knows that they'll be having a particularly difficult conversation with a direct report or a peer, they may prepare by creating bullet points of the issues that need to be covered. While this is always helpful, it may not be until you articulate the bullets into more complete thoughts that you get a true sense of the impact, order, choice, or emphasis that each point needs. Role play with a partner can be helpful, but may not always be practical, so doing a "solo" role play can be used. In cases like this, role play can be employed almost anytime, anywhere. A learner can always practice in their head, without much notice. However, a better approach may be to conduct the role play out loud and do so in your car, the shower, or any private space where you will not be interrupted or overheard. Regardless of what you're role playing about on your own or with a partner, there are some logical steps to follow and ways to prepare.

Worksheet 6.2 lays out the information that you will need to plan a more formal role play rather than one that occurs on the spur of the moment. To start,

Worksheet 6.2 Role Play Planner

Competency/situation/skill to practice:	Date:
Objective:	
Date, time, and location of role play:	
Describe role play scenario:	
Partners, if any; roles for each partner:	
Preparation needed:	
Materials, if any, needed:	

Observers:	Facilitator:
Organizational factors to consider:	**Personal factors to consider:**

Table 6.2 Debrief Questions for Post Role Play Review

---

1. What are 2–3 things you thought went well in the role play that allowed you to learn?
2. What are 2–3 things that did not go smoothly in the role play; why did this occur and what did you learn from them?
3. Were there any "Aha" moments where you gained insight into your behavior as to why you said or did something that was effective? Or, conversely, ineffective?
4. What will you do differently when the actual scenario takes place that you didn't do in the role play?
5. What won't you do in the actual scenario that you found was ineffective in the role play?
6. Did you have the right material in front of you or was there something else you need to do to prepare?
7. Each role play partner should be asked to evaluate your skills and performance and be encouraged to offer honest and constructive feedback.
8. What was supposed to happen in the scenario and did it occur? If you were practicing delegating a task, was this accomplished; if it was coaching an employee, did this occur effectively?
9. Was the tone of the role play what you expected? Did the discussion progress as you expected?
10. Should the role play be tried again? With the same partners or different partners?

---

you will need to consider the skill or situation you want to practice and then capture the context. For example, where did the situation you want to practice take place or where will it take place? You can practice something that occurred in the past to be better at it in the future. Or, you can practice something in advance to be better prepared for the situation when it does occur. If the role play will be done with partners, describe the roles each will play and capture any instructions for them about their role. Indicate any preparation or materials that may be needed (e.g., review or read materials). In addition to identifying your objective, context, and materials, once the role play has been conducted you need to conduct a debrief. A debrief provides a feedback loop so that you and your role play partners can discuss what happened in the role play and what you can learn from it. Table 6.2 suggests some debrief questions.

When to Use Role Play

Regardless of the skill that you are trying to develop, there are a number of factors that can be identified to help you determine if role play, individually or in partnership, will be a good idea for developing your identified competency. If any of the following conditions exist, using a role play can be beneficial:

- When you're uncertain of what reactions you may get from others
- The situation has many complexities
- When you feel some trepidation going into a situation
- When you simply want to practice
- When empathy and understanding need to be developed

- When you want feedback
- The need to practice a direct confrontation exists
- When there is a need to get "unstuck"
- When articulating your end of the conversation will be helpful
- When you want to develop confidence
- If there is a need for fluidity and clear delivery

As you can see from this list, role play can be used to both develop a new competency and to gain comfort and skill with existing competencies. Role play can be used for a wide variety of scenarios and it is supportive of a self-directed learning approach.

When Not to Use Role Play

While there are many benefits to role play and situations when using role play makes good sense, there are also times when using role play may be ineffective or not worth the investment of time or effort. As a self-directed learner you need to be able to analyze your needs and match your learning tools to those needs. If the following conditions exist, using a role play may not be beneficial:

- Time needed to prepare for role play is not available
- Time needed to practice and debrief is not available
- May not have willing or able role play partners
- Role play on your own may be helpful but will not provide needed feedback
- Role play partner may not be comfortable giving honest feedback
- Potential for high emotions exists
- May practice poor behaviors
- There is no instruction offered
- May be incompatible for learner's style
- May be uncomfortable for learner
- May be uncomfortable for the partner
- Role play partner is not enough of a subject matter expert

Making the decision not to conduct a role play can be important because you do not want to risk reinforcing the wrong behavior or asking for assistance that ends up putting a strain on your relationship with the partner you've selected.

Role Play Scenarios

Role play scenario opportunities can pop up at any point in time. Getting into the habit of role play can allow a learner to develop the skill and comfort to slip into this mode quickly and easily. One way to accomplish this is to build a learning plan that includes regular role play activities. Ideas for role play exist for all managers – even if you're an individual contributor or work remotely. Managers often need practice and skill in delivering messages, instructions, and feedback. It should be fairly easy to identify role play opportunities once you begin to think about

Table 6.3 Practice Role Play Scenarios

- Accepting praise for a job well done
- Asking for an explanation of something
- Assigning tasks
- Budget discussion
- Comfort with collegial interaction, interpersonal skills
- Congratulate an employee for an accomplishment
- Delivering an important organizational message
- Employee not taking initiative
- Encourage a team to meet a deadline
- IT discussion about resource allocation
- Late employee
- Poor performer, coaching
- Proactive networking
- Request for task force assignment
- Thanking an employee for their initiative
- Too much work from supervisor
- Visiting expatriate from Europe
- Work-life balance, coach an employee about work life

the benefits and how easy the application of a role play can be in day-to-day activities. Table 6.3 provides some general ideas and is by no means an exhaustive list. It should be noted, <u>not</u> all of the scenarios are problems. In fact, practicing positive behaviors is as important as practicing difficult scenarios. Table 6.4 provides ten competency scenarios plus one skill combination scenario for practicing. As managers, we need to ensure engagement and commitment and this means being effective at praise and positive feedback as well as collective or difficult conversations.

Developing Role Play Scenarios for Future Use

Each week we encounter different situations. Some are routine and others are unique or provide opportunities for stress or learning. As a way to prepare for these situations and practice through role play, think ahead and identify role play scenarios that you can do. Start by checking your calendar on Sunday night or Monday morning for possible role play scenarios. Look for situations that may occur where you can benefit from practicing. Be conscious of where/when you need to practice and which competencies you are trying to develop. Chart out your role play activities for the week. You can also plan ahead for specific milestone events such as performance reviews, budget planning, or other organizational initiatives. In addition, you can plan role play events independently to coincide with a particular skill that you are trying to develop. For an illustration, see Example 6.1 which shows how Chris, our senior manager, will approach a role play learning plan about *change management* that she needs to do to help her prepare for her role after the acquisition.

Table 6.4 Ten Sample Role Play Scenarios by Competency

Coaching:	Jenna, a colleague, wants to advance in the company. She's bright but needs lots of help in understanding how to navigate the politics that occurs periodically in your organization.
Building teams:	A team on which you sit is dysfunctional and the primary reason stems from poor communication and follow-through from members; most act like individual contributors rather than as a team.
Analytical thinking:	Take a piece of data about your business – turnover, sales, or any key performance indicator. With a partner, who also knows your business, role play with you explaining the data and what it means.
Organization awareness:	One of your employees seems unaware of other organization priorities; it is affecting your other staff. Role play a discussion that is targeted at uncovering the reasons and which is designed to work through possible solutions with the employee.
Building relationships:	Practice your approach to meeting new people in a networking environment that repeats monthly and where seeing other participants regularly is likely.
Business acumen:	A friend of yours wants to advance in his organization; you are concerned for him that he does not have the vocabulary and general business sense that he needs. You think reading business publications regularly will be very helpful. Explain why business acumen is important for your friend.
Change management:	The employee handbook in your organization has just been updated with lots of changes – especially in how vacation is accrued. You need to roll this out to your staff.
Adaptability:	Recently your boss told you that you weren't as adaptable as you needed to be on a project change that was handed down from a few levels up. She tells you to expect more changes in the coming months.
Collaboration:	Peter, another manager at your level, tends to look at things from his functional lens and does not partner well; you have a new project that will require working with him and his team.
Accountability:	Your employee, Derek, has been asked by you to develop and produce a new report on a monthly basis. You've delegated other things to Derek in the past but for some reason he will not accept accountability for this assignment. As a result, your own accountability is being questioned when the report is delayed each month.
Combination scenario for multiple competencies: • **Influencing others** • **Building commitment** • **Human capital management** • **Team building**	Your team is working on a new project and you've asked all your staff to come into the office for a kick-off meeting and then regular staff meetings in the office every two weeks. The project is critical and you believe the team needs face-to-face meetings, at least in the kick-off phase over three months. You have an employee who telecommutes every day; your organization has a policy for remote workers that sets out equipment, logistics, and other key requirements. Anna, your telecommuting employee, has pushed back in a big way – she doesn't want to come into the office every two weeks and is insisting that if you make it a requirement, she wants to be paid for coming into the office, including a stipend for transportation. You're dumbfounded by this demand. Although not explicit in the company telecommuting policy, this is not something your organization will do. Role play how you will influence Anna to change her view – and do so without creating a contentious situation or one that will result in losing Anna or negativity affecting her productivity, which is quite good. You must also preserve the team focus.

Example 6.1 Role Play Planner – Chris

Competency/situation/skill to practice: *Change management*	Date: *November 2020*

Objective: *To prepare for the pending merger/acquisition and the changes that will follow, prepare to understand and accept change for myself and my team and prepare to lead change throughout the organization.*

Date, time, and location of role play: *Series of weekly role play events starting this month, November, and commencing for the next three months until the merger is complete.*

Describe role play scenarios:

1. *Review processes and suggest ways to streamline them and integrate with the new organization*
2. *Describe new organization culture and role play about the differences between the organizations*
3. *Role play interactions with customers/clients telling them about the acquisition*
4. *Role play internal communication events discussing the changes to come*
5. *Look for potential role play issues as more information is rolled out over the next three months*

Partners, if any; roles for each partner:

1. *Spouse and professional friends/colleagues in the early stages*
2. *Other senior leaders in the organization in the mid-stages*
3. *My team members as we get closer to the acquisition date*

Preparation needed:

1. *Research new organization as much as possible; seek out employees at the company through my network*
2. *Look at job board sites like Glassdoor for insights into their culture*
3. *Study all their products and research where the overlap is, if any, to our products and services*
4. *Learn about change management itself; what are the drivers and what are the barriers*
5. *Find and talk with leaders in other organizations who have been through a similar acquisition*

Materials, if any, needed:

1. *Annual reports and other public data from the acquisition; all internal e-mails about acquisition*
2. *Employee attitude survey results from the previous few years to look for potential pain points*

Observers: *Potentially have staff observe as other managers and I role play; think about including my boss at a later stage*	Facilitator: *Not sure if this will be needed; consider for the later stages*

Organizational factors to consider:	Personal factors to consider:
1. *Staff are very nervous right now* 2. *Rumors have been flying* 3. *Some staff are job searching already*	1. *I don't want to leave this job* 2. *Worried that my skillset will not be a match* 3. *Have been doing my job pretty much the same way for a long time*

Improving Role Play Effectiveness: Tips for Success

A role play can be impromptu, quick, and easy. Getting into the habit of playing scenes in your head or briefly with a partner can be quite helpful. Planning out your role plays will be more effective if you consider some of the following factors. Self-directed learning allows for a person to create meaningful role plays outside of formal training and education programs. The following tips may help you to create more successful role play interactions.

Do advance planning. Write out the roles and think about all the potential bumps that can occur. Have all the information and documents that you may need. If the scenario being practiced has a specific day and time think through any issues with respect to nuances that can influence the role play. In short, the more planning you do in advance the smoother your role play is likely to go.

Imitate actual scenarios. Write a good plot. If your role play is not a specific event like a presentation to executives but rather is meant as general practice for something like providing feedback to an employee or disciplining an employee, be sure to write out or plan all the pertinent details. Make sure you have all the details you may need to recreate the scenario such as performance data or other relevant documents. You may also wish to think about things like what day of the week or month the likely interaction will take place. For example, some days of the week may be different due to telecommuting schedules and some days of the month may have implications for monthly reports or other busy times.

Engage willing participants. If you have options as to the partners you engage in your role play, think about the fit the individual brings to the exercise and whether or not they will be engaged in your learning journey. Some partners will be more than happy to participate and assist while others may, for whatever reason, not be engaged in your quest. To ensure that participants are willing, be sure to explain why you would like to conduct the role play and what you hope to gain by completing it. Ask directly if this is something they are willing to do or how they might approach the situation. Going ahead with a role play that you can see will be a strain may have negative consequences with respect to your practice and confidence. It may be better to role play on your own, with less feedback, than to go ahead with a negative interaction.

Define what effective behavior looks like. What behaviors are you looking to display? How do you want to behave differently or who might you wish to emulate? For example, if you are trying to develop your coaching competency or skills in dealing with pressure, the behaviors you want to display may include being calm, clear, and level-headed. You may want to identify behaviors like: remain positive, listen carefully, focus on setting goals, etc. Having an idea of what behaviors will match with your objective will ensure that you work toward that outcome.

Consider using an observer. In addition to a partner who may play a role in your role play, think about including an observer whose role is to simply watch what you do as well as how the partner reacts to you. This person can take notes, make observations after the fact, and offer suggestions that someone who is directly participating in the role play may not be able to do. If additional practice is desired or called for then the observer can switch roles with the partner and react in ways that may be different and quite helpful.

Engage a facilitator. Like an observer, a facilitator is a neutral third party who can help the role play flow more effectively. A facilitator can be the one who calls for a pause or rewind and can also encourage a role play to go down an additional path if it appears that this will be helpful. The facilitator can also give direction to both the partner and the learner in an effort to assist or make things progress more smoothly. A facilitator, unlike an observer, will likely need a bit more skill to foster additional learning. Facilitators may not always be helpful but in situations where there are more complexities or high emotions a facilitator can be useful.

Pause and rewind. If the role play is awkward or does not seem to be working, it's perfectly acceptable to take a break or interrupt the scene. Try to figure out what the problem is or simply state that you want to take a different approach. Rewinding may not be something you can do in an actual scenario but this is one of the advantages of a role play where you can try something different or acknowledge when something is not working well.

Location. Whenever possible, use the actual location or environment in which the work situation will take place. Plan the rehearsal for a time when you will not be noticed or disrupted by others. For example, if you wish to role play a presentation to a top executive or important client, use the conference room where the presentation is likely to take place. Make sure any equipment you may be using will work properly and stand or sit where you are likely to be for the presentation. You can do a role play like this on your own, or with partners who can provide feedback or simulate the questions you may receive.

Video tape or audio tape. Consider taping the role play with either audio or video, or both. This will be especially helpful if you are role playing on your own as it will provide you with a tangible source of feedback. If you have partners it will also be helpful during a debrief to discuss both verbal and nonverbal behaviors.

Always conduct a debrief. After a role play or set of role plays sit back and review what happened. Examine what went well and what did not. Ask yourself what you might have done differently and ask your role play partners, if there are any, what feedback they have. Press for details and consider all possible angles. Think about both content and process. Consider both facts and emotions. You may, if you have time, jot down questions or concerns while the role play is occurring. In the end, you want to talk about what happened in the role play in addition to the practice it provides.

Repeat. If time permits and partners are willing, consider repeating the scene. Each time the role play is replicated you can try emphasizing different words, using different tones, or using different verbiage all together. Repeating may also allow you to practice, perhaps even memorize the words or phrases that you want to use. If there is a particular message that needs to be conveyed or there are specific words that need to be used, practicing more than once will help them to become easier to say and may allow the interaction to come across as more natural.

Notes

1 https://roleplayasaninstructionalmethodforadultlearners.weebly.com/
2 www.instructure.com/bridge/blog/10-stats-about-learning-retention-youll-want-forget?newhome=bridge
3 www.unb.ca/fredericton/cetl/tls/resources/teaching_tips/tt_instructional_methods/effective_scenarios.html
4 https://bizfluent.com/info-12027484-advantages-disadvantages-using-role-play-training-method.html
5 www.mindtools.com/CommSkll/RolePlaying.htm

Bibliography

Bingham, M. (Retrieved May, 2019). 10 Stats About Learning Retention You'll Want to Forget. Available: www.instructure.com/bridge/blog/10-stats-about-learning-retention-youll-want-forget?newhome=bridge

Center for Enhanced Teaching and Learning (Retrieved June, 2019). Creating Effective Scenarios, Case Studies, and Role Plays. Available: www.unb.ca/fredericton/cetl/tls/resources/teaching_tips/tt_instructional_methods/effective_scenarios.html

Ching, Y. H. (2014). Exploring the Impact of Role-Playing on Peer Feedback in an Online Case-Based Learning Activity. *The International Journal of Research in Open and Distributed Learning*, Vol. 15, No. 3.

Mind Tools (Retrieved July, 2019). Role-Playing: Preparing for Difficult Conversations and Situations. Available: www.mindtools.com/CommSkll/RolePlaying.htm

Role Play as an Instructional Method for Adult Learners (Retrieved May, 2019). Available: https://roleplayasaninstructionalmethodforadultlearners.weebly.com/

Salas, E., Wildman, J., and Piccolo, R. (2009). Using Simulation-Based Training to Enhance Management Education. *Academy of Management Learning & Education*, Vol. 8, No. 4, 559–573.

Thompson, J. (2018). Advantages & Disadvantages for Using Role Play as a Training Method. Available: https://bizfluent.com/info-12027484-advantages-disadvantages-using-role-play-training-method.html

7 The Art of Questioning

On-the-job experience provides exposure to managerial behavior. By doing, observing, and interacting, you learn what to do or not do – and, over time, you develop your own style. These experiences can profoundly shape who you are as a manager. Do you always understand what you see or agree with what you observe? Oftentimes learning comes from reflecting on what you've seen, heard, or heard about. The developing manager needs to be introspective about their experience in order to codify a set of rules or behaviors for themselves. The best way to do this is through questions and feedback – and while feedback about specific behaviors is important, it is also helpful to get feedback on managerial behaviors in general. What better way to do this than through asking questions and listening?

Asking questions is an everyday occurrence. We ask how people are doing, for cream with our coffee, for a coworker to assist with something, for a vacation day to go on the schedule, and for a little more gravy on our turkey. Sometimes we give little to no thought about these questions; they pop into our head and roll off our tongue. Other times, we are more thoughtful about our questions, formulating them in our minds or writing/rewriting them in an e-mail or other communication. Although questions are commonplace, most of us do not realize the power of a question. A powerful question strategy can get you something you want, and can also make a point to the recipient. We all have the capacity to drive our learning journey with questions.

Critical Thinking

Socrates, who was a Greek philosopher, tried to understand fundamental viewpoints by asking questions. His goal was to find a contradiction or an inflection point. His purpose was to develop critical thinking skills in his students. The "Socratic method," therefore, is the concept of asking and answering questions for the purpose of eliciting and developing critical thinking or objective analysis. In fact, today the Socratic method is thought of as a powerful teaching method and is thought of as a highly disciplined process.[1] Using this method allows both the questioner and the respondent to develop their thinking on a particular topic or issue. The idea behind the Socratic method is that you use a specific set of questions to lead the learner down a path toward learning a new idea or approach.

Applying this methodology to the development of managerial competencies, the learner can be both the teacher and the learner at the same time.

Once your learning priorities have been identified through a self-assessment, you can apply these priorities in a variety of ways. A good place to start is with a list of questions you want to have answered. If one of your priorities happens to be to develop a *global mindset*, consider the way well-planned and well-placed questions can assist you in your learning journey. One way to start is by listing the things you'd like to know or the things you're aware of that you don't know. Second, you'll probably want to do some reading on the subject and, third, talk to a few folks you know who are more knowledgeable on the subject. Much of this can be done through networking, as discussed in Chapter 5. From here, you can start building a comprehensive set of questions as well as a plan for who to ask and when. For example, with the *global mindset* competency, some key questions might be:

- What are the key things a person should do to develop a global mindset?
- How do you know when you have a global mindset?
- How can you develop a global mindset?
- What resources might you suggest I use/consider?
- Who are some good examples of people in my organization who have a global mindset?
- Who are some examples of people in business who display a global mindset?
- What behaviors do people with a global mindset display?
- What behaviors do people with a global mindset avoid?
- I haven't traveled internationally that much; will this hamper my development of a global mindset and is there anything I can do about it?

Recall Example 5.1 where Dara created a networking plan to help her develop a *global mindset*. The focus of the example was on networking and only a few questions were identified in the example. Chances are Dara had this more detailed list of questions in mind for her more in-depth interviews. The questions are still relatively broad. There will be more questions specific to you and your need to develop a global mindset – such as the specific reasons why this is a priority for you. For instance, if you have an upcoming temporary assignment in Dubai, your questions may be more specific to the country and the region. Similar broad questions could be used or applied to different competencies. There are many different question types to choose from. Open versus closed, hypothetical, probing, and others offer different ways for a questioner to seek information. Table 7.1 identifies the various question types which exist.

How to Engage in a Questioning Strategy

Developing the questions may actually be the easy part of employing questioning as a learning strategy. The more difficult part may be in how you go about getting answers. Some of the *global mindset* questions above can't really be answered by a single person if you expect to ensure learning. Often you need to seek input from

Table 7.1 Types of Questions

• Choice questions	• Open question
• Clarification question	• Probing question
• Closed question	• Questions about the question
• Evaluative question	• Recall question
• Factual question	• Research question
• Funneling questions	• Rhetorical questions
• Hypothetical question	• Tag questions
• Indirect question	• Wh-questions (e.g., who, what, where, why, etc.)
• Interpretive question	
• Leading/loaded question	• Yes/No questions

multiple people, with a variety of perspectives, in order to start formulating your own view and your own style. How many people do you have to ask: "How do you know when you have a global mindset?" There's no set rule or magical number. You can ask three people the same question and get three different perspectives. So, when do you know if you've asked enough people the same question? One rule of thumb could be when you start seeing patterns or getting similar answers. Another rule of thumb can be when you start feeling like there is a style or approach that seems to fit with who you are as a person and as a manager.

You can be more scientific in your data collection by writing notes about the answers to your questions so you can begin to group the responses into categories or themes. You will want to also categorize respondents by some key demographics too – women compared to men, those who have lived abroad and those who have not, those who have traveled extensively and those who have not, those inside your organization and those outside your organization, etc. This will allow you to see if there are meaningful differences and/or meaningful themes. These comparisons also imply that you will want to be thoughtful about how you develop your interview pool. Asking questions can be formal or informal and what you do with the information you collect may be the difference between whether or not you are able to internalize the information and learn.

Informal Versus Formal Question Strategy

There is power in the act of asking questions because the exchange can go far beyond a simple discussion or sharing of information. You can approach asking questions in a very informal way, or, using a more formal strategy. Some combination of the two is best for more robust learning. On the informal side, you should have a broad set of questions in mind for each of the competencies you'd like to develop. It is a good idea to write these down and/or capture them in a place that is easily accessible such as your favorite folio or on an e-device that you usually carry with you. You're not going to ask every person you encounter all of these questions but you should have some strategy as to who you might ask what questions, and under what circumstances. For instance, if you go to lunch with a colleague and meet someone from his or her network, you can casually bring up the topic of global travel or global assignments. If you learn that this person has some expertise in this area, ask a few of your questions. If it looks like this person has a lot of expertise or insight, you can request to have coffee or lunch with them for the purpose of a deeper conversation. This is a great way to combine networking with questions. There are many instances when informally asking questions will work. Take into account that you always want to have your questions in mind and a plan for how to capture the information.

On the more formal side you may wish to build a plan for identifying an array of people to talk with to ask your questions. How many people you identify and how many you actually engage may depend on how deep your need is or how immediate your need. Worksheet 7.1 provides some ideas on how to organize your question campaign. First, consider whether there are people from whom you think you can learn compared to those who you think may be more helpful in confirming your interpretation of what you've learned. From a self-directed learner perspective, you need both. Some people may serve both purposes and others may fit in a single category or the other. As the worksheet suggests, there are many categories of potential question targets to consider.

Consider different types of people who may be a good source of learning. For example, are there experts or other subject matter experts (SMEs) that you know? Are there people you know who are knowledgeable about the competency you wish to develop and who can recommend others? Do you have coworkers or peers, both inside and outside your organization, who may be insightful? Are there bosses, either current or former, or other executives in your organization who you can consider? The best strategy is to write down as many names as you can think of to establish an all-inclusive list. Next, prioritize the names by thinking about who you honestly think will be the most helpful and whether or not you think they will be responsive to your request for an information/ informal interview. Casting a wide net in the planning stage will ensure that you end up with a diverse and knowledgeable pool. Consider this worksheet as a living document that you modify as needed. Save your worksheets because you may be able to consider some of the people for more than one competency development plan.

Types of Questions

There are many different types of questions that can be employed across a wide variety of settings and purposes. Some questions are simple, straightforward, and take little thought or effort on the part of the respondent. Other questions are more complex and require a bit more thought or introspection on the part of the respondent. As shown in Table 7.1, there are a variety of types of questions. Table 7.2 provides brief definitions of the range of question types that exist[2] along with application examples. For the purpose of learning and developing managerial competencies there are a few question types that may be more useful than others. There are some question types which will be of limited or no value to you as you gather information and learn. It is not necessary for you to identify the exact type of question as you build your question guide, however, it can be useful as you begin to think about what you want to learn and from whom you want to learn.

Worksheet 7.1 Building a Plan for Questioning

	Learn	*Confirm*
• Experts/SME		
• Coworkers • Peers inside/outside organization		

• Bosses current
  and former
• Senior managers and
  executives		

• People you meet
  through others
• People you meet
  networking		

Table 7.2 Question Type Definitions and Applications

Question Type	Example
Choice Question Yes/No Question	Designed to provide you with a specific answer: • "Do you prefer <u>Harvard Business Review</u> or <u>McKinsey Quarterly</u> to build your *business acumen*?" • "Which do you find more valuable for developing *business acumen* – the <u>Wall Street Journal</u> or the <u>Financial Times</u>?" • "Is the <u>Wall Street Journal</u> the best publication to read to develop my *business acumen*?"
Clarification Question	Intended to get more information or an explanation: • "The other day I heard you talking about *resilience* to changing business needs as a way to be more adaptable; can you tell me what you mean by that?" • "I've heard you say that *adaptability* is an important competency for any manager; is this because our work assignments change so much?"
Closed Question	Designed to elicit a brief, yet specific response: • "What are the top 2 or 3 managerial competencies that new managers should develop?" • "What are the 2 or 3 managerial competencies that you think change the most over time?" • "What are the 1 or 2 more difficult managerial competencies to develop?"

(continued)

Table 7.2 (Cont.)

Question Type	Example
Evaluative Question	Looking for a more developed and insightful response: • "How is a concern for *risk-taking* incorporated into product development?" • "How do you balance cost containment with a concern for *risk-taking*?" • "Is a concern for quality the most important aspect of customer service and how do you measure this aspect of *risk-taking*?"
Factual Question	Looking for a straightforward and accurate response: • "Does this organization have a statement about *ethics*?" • "Is *ethics* a part of the stated values of the organization?" • "Have there been sanctions for *ethical* violations in the past year?"
Funneling Question	Series of questions that start broad and get successively specific: • "Tell me about how you *motivate* employees?" • "What have you found to be effective with more seasoned employees?" • "Which strategy worked the best for this group of employees?" • "Are there certain conditions under which this *motivational* strategy worked better?" • "Did you try this strategy with other groups of employees?"
Hypothetical Question	Poses a supposed situation to get at a person's knowledge or approach to something: • "What would you do if you had an employee who you didn't *trust*?" • "What would you do if you suspected an employee of breaking your *trust*?" • "How would you handle a situation if you thought an employee had violated your confidence?"
Indirect Question	A question inside of a statement; not as applicable to self-directed learning: • "I wonder if *stress* is as much of a derailment as people say it is?" • "They don't know how to address whether or not this was *stress*." • "I wonder how much of a role *stress* played in this situation?"
Interpretive Question	A question that may not have a specific answer; can be extremely useful for collecting opinions and multiple approaches: • "It seems like this group is not acting like a *collaborative* team; what do you think the reasons are for this failure?" • "This group seems dysfunctional; what do you think are the causes?" • "I've tried to instill a sense of *collaboration* with this team but have not been successful; do you have any ideas about why?"

Table 7.2 (Cont.)

Question Type	Example
Leading/Loaded Question	There's no real application for learning with these types of questions – they tend to hint at the answer in the question or contain false or misleading information in the question.
Open Question	Allow for longer responses and potentially more information: • "How do you find time to be *innovative*?" • "What are some of the things you do to be *innovative*?" • "How do you know when to use an *innovative* solution rather than one that has been used in the past?" • "Can you explain when you know something is truly *innovative*?"
Probing Question	Designed to solicit additional information: • "When you *delegate* a task to a direct report, how often do you follow up to see that it's done and do you differentiate based on who it is?" • "That's great advice regarding *delegating* tasks; can you give me some examples of when that's worked the best?" • "Has that approach to *delegating* ever given you problems or not worked with certain people?" And of course: • Tell me more…? • For instance? • Can you give me an example…? • How so? • Can you give me more details? • What was your role? • How did your boss react? • What did you do next? • What are you implying? • Are there any generalizations you can make?
Question About the Question	Used to gain clarification or to explain something: • "Why do you think I asked you that question?" • "What's the point of asking that question?"
Recall Question	Although you may use recall questions on a day-to-day basis – such as, "What was the dollar amount we committed to raise?" – these questions are less helpful from a Socratic method perspective or from a self-directed learning perspective.
Research Question	A research question is a technical question that seeks to find a specific answer based on either qualitative or quantitative data collection. For the purpose of developing managerial competencies you might use questions like the ones highlighted in the "Closed Question" box above. With this type of question, you are not conducting the "research" for others, but rather, yourself.

(continued)

Table 7.2 (Cont.)

Question Type	Example
Rhetorical Question	This type of question is typically asked for effect rather than to seek a specific answer; "Will you join me in this important mission?" It is not likely to be a question type that will assist with your learning journey.
Tag Question	This is a small question mainly used at the end of a sentence with the goal of confirming something: • "You're an expert *negotiator*, aren't you?" • "That was a stressful *negotiation*, wasn't it?"
Wh-question	Uses an interrogative to stipulate the information desired; also, a form of open questioning: • Who • What • Where • Why • When • Which • How

Building a Question Strategy

Regardless of the type of question you write or ask, it will be important to develop a strategy for how you approach building your learning plan using questions. One way of thinking about this is that you are aiming for a target. Your overall objective is to accomplish your learning goals for a single competency that you wish to develop. You may have multiple targets because there are multiple competencies that you wish to develop. Thinking about each competency individually will allow for more focused learning. There may be overlap in the subject matter experts (SMEs) who can assist you in learning what you want to learn; however, for the purpose of building a focused plan for each competency, it is a good idea to build separate plans for each competency.

Figure 7.1 shows that building a question strategy *is* a targeted process. The outermost ring of your target is where you begin. You may have some general questions or even a few more specific ones but your purpose is to explore the competency that you wish to develop. Before you can ask a lot of perceptive questions you need to have a strong foundation that helps you form the basis for your understanding and your ability to delve deeper with your inquiry. In this early stage of inquiry, you may be asking for resources to review and people to approach who may be able to help you. The next group out from the target will also be SMEs but these individuals may or may not have the same level of expertise as the SMEs at the center. It could also be that these individuals simply have less time to give you or are more difficult to reach or interact with. Your questions will be specific and focused and may be designed to elicit information

Targeted

Deeper questions

SMEs

Focused

Specific questions

Seeking information and names

General

Curiosity/Exploration

Seeking resources

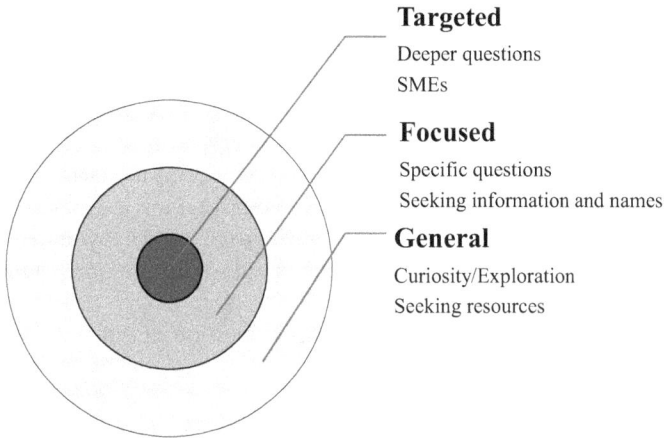

Figure 7.1 Sequencing a Question Strategy

and recommendations for additional people with whom to speak. It is possible that a person in the center ring could also be at the center of the target but it is likely that you will want to ask your questions in a sequence so that you can apply what you learn at each point in the strategy. At the center of the target will be the SMEs who can offer you the most insights and who can discuss with you your viewpoint and approach to the skill that you're trying to master. With these individuals you will be learning and confirming your knowledge and you may have an opportunity to practice what you know through conversation. Your questions will be deeper and more strategic with this group and you may also be directed to additional resources.

As you build your question strategy there are a number of factors to consider. It may make sense to start with a blank sheet of paper and begin to list what you want to know. However, until you start to talk with people and learn about the parameters of the competency you want to learn, you may not be able to articulate specific questions. Starting with some basic reading and research on the topic will be helpful. In order to build your sequence of questions and identify people to talk with it makes sense to have a way to think about who you should seek out for further discussion.

Who to Target

Talking with one person, or even just a few, may or may not get you the tools that you need to build your expertise. Building your expertise will involve both learning and confirming what you know as well as providing an opportunity to practice some of the skills or have deeper discussions about the application of behaviors in different environments. Moreover, you will want to think about who has the time to help you, who has the inclination to invest in you, and who has the expertise you seek. Worksheet 7.1, presented earlier, provides a way to approach the development of your list of who to engage for your question strategy. As you think about who to include and the various question types available, also consider the following:

- What type of questions work best for what you want to learn?
- Which questions should be asked first in your learning journey?
- Are there questions you need to ask in order to frame what you need to learn?
- Who should be asked which questions or subset of questions? How do you determine this?
- How many times should you ask the same question of different people?
- How do you know when to probe?

Worksheet 7.2 provides a way to follow a targeted questions strategy (Figure 7.1). Writing down your initial questions will allow you to think through what you already know and what you need to know by starting with general questions, becoming more focused, and ending with deeper and more sophisticated questions that are designed to help you learn.

Example 7.1 provides an example of how this worksheet might look in practice. Recall Nick, our individual contributor from Chapter 2. Nick would like to advance in his organization and career. He knows that being able to give feedback and receive it will be very important. He'd like to focus on this competency and has developed an initial set of questions to help him find out more about feedback and how he can become better at both giving and receiving feedback.

A question strategy involves developing good questions and identifying the right people from whom to seek answers. The process involves holding a series of interviews. Networking can help you identify who to interview but the nature of a question strategy is such that it moves you into a deeper interview exchange and goes beyond an initial networking encounter.

Improving a Question Strategy: Tips for Success

Some of the distinct advantages of this learning tool are that questions can be easily combined with other tools such as networking or observation. Additionally, a question strategy can also be combined with external activities such as attending conferences, seminars, or other training activities. Another advantage is that preparing questions can itself be an opportunity for learning. Thinking through what to ask, who to ask, and even where to ask can be insightful. The act of asking questions will provide practice and learning. Seeing and hearing reactions can be informative. One more advantage of questioning is that it can be relatively low in cost. You may need to invest in a meal or a drink or perhaps a registration fee for an event but these are low-cost and will offer a good return on investment. Finally, questioning of multiple people by its nature will be spread out over time. This is an advantage because it gives learning an opportunity to germinate and be reinforced.

Worksheet 7.2 Question Development

Competency:	Date:

General Questions: Think about the broad questions you have and the resources you need.
1.

2.

3.

4.

5.

6.

Focused Questions: Write down more specific questions about the competency and think about including a request for names of people who can assist.
1.

2.

3.

4.

5.

6.

Targeted Questions: Construct deep and more complex questions to ask SMEs; you may assign some questions to specific individuals or you may ask the same question of multiple people.
1.

2.

3.

4.

5.

6.

Instructions: Use as many worksheets as necessary to capture your questions. You may also want to note if the questions are designed for a particular audience or type of individual to ensure that you have enough variety in who you interview.

Sequence questions effectively. Be thoughtful about which questions to ask and in what order. Keep in mind that you can change the sequence for certain targets based upon what you know about them or based upon previous people you've already interviewed. Think about starting with easier or shorter questions and moving on to more complex or sophisticated questions.

Example 7.1 Nick's Questions

Competency: Feedback	**Date:** 9/15/2020

General Questions: Think about the broad questions you have and the resources you need.

1. *Does feedback always need to be negative or constructive?*

2. *Why do so many people get nervous about giving feedback to someone else?*

3. *Is there a professional way to accept feedback – even if you're not sure it will be helpful?*

4. *Is there a time when you shouldn't try to give feedback?*

5. *Why do people think feedback is so important?*

Focused Questions: Write down more specific questions about the competency and think about including a request for names of people who can assist.

1. *I was recently given feedback about my career by a coworker; I'm OK that she did this but it was unsolicited and I was not sure how to react. What do you do in a case like this?*

2. *Do you have any resources that you might suggest for learning more about feedback? Any YouTube videos, books, websites, or articles that I should consider?*

3. *Is there anyone here in our organization that you think delivers feedback particularly well who I can talk with – anyone who struggles with giving feedback?*

4. *Are there certain phrases to avoid when giving feedback? Any phrases that work well?*

5. *What do you do if someone gets angry or upset when you give them feedback?*

Targeted Questions: Construct deep and more complex questions to ask SMEs; you may assign some questions to specific individuals or you may ask the same question of multiple people.

1. *I've heard the phrase "feedback is a gift." Why do you think this is the case – or do you disagree?*

2. *Since I'm not yet a supervisor I don't have a lot of opportunity to provide feedback to others from a work perspective? How would you suggest I start to build this skill so I can be prepared to supervise?*

3. *What are the 2 or 3 things that you have seen work well when you've watched others give feedback to someone or when you've given feedback?*

4. *What are the 2 or 3 things that tend to derail a conversation when feedback is being provided?*

5. *How do you balance the need to provide feedback to someone with the high emotions that can sometimes be present in a feedback situation?*

Framing. In addition to framing a question so that it is clear to the recipient what your objective is in asking the question, also be prepared to frame your underlying learning objective. It may be helpful for the recipient to know why you are seeking the information and how you will use it. Most people will be more relaxed and open if they know you are on a personal learning journey rather than fulfilling some other business requirement.

Ask follow-up questions. Do not hesitate to ask follow-up questions. That is, be cautious not to get too tied to your list of questions without taking the time to probe an answer or have more of a discussion with someone who is an expert or who can provide you with insights. Having established questions is important but being overly focused on the list can result in a missed opportunity to delve deeper into something that may prove to be helpful.

Write it down. Take notes whenever possible and if not possible in the moment, write notes as soon as possible after the discussion so you capture the detail, not just the essence of what's being shared. Approaching your SME and targets as an interview will make it much easier to take notes. Most people when asked if it's OK to take notes will say yes.

Open-ended versus closed questions. Try not to assume that certain questions must be asked as open versus closed. If you ask a question in an open way and are not getting the feedback you think will be helpful, try rephrasing the question to be closed. The reverse may hold true as well. If there is a particular piece of information that you seek, try preparing both a closed and an open question so that you can modify the approach if necessary. For example: closed – "If I'm traveling to Spain on business, is it important that I be able to speak Spanish?" Open – "What has been your experience with how receptive people are to those who travel to Spain on business who don't speak Spanish?"

Drawing out the target. At times you may find it necessary to encourage or perhaps even persuade someone to share their thoughts or perspectives on an issue you are trying to learn. Expressing their ideas on something may be difficult – even if they are an SME, or it may be difficult for them to express feelings on something that is sensitive or even viewed as personal. In a case like this, pulling out or extracting information may take some additional finesse to induce someone to speak freely. Assuring someone of your purpose and that you will not reveal their name (if this is a concern for them) or use the information for anything other than your personal learning may be important to do. Thanking someone and complimenting them on their knowledge, skills, or abilities may help in this situation. Your sentiment must, however, be genuine.

The power of silence. Most people tend to be uncomfortable with silence when they are in a conversation or when they ask a question and there is no immediate response. Oftentimes, what may actually be only a few seconds or even just half a minute, seems like a huge gap. However, it could be that the recipient of the question is gathering their thoughts before responding. Tamp down your fear that you've asked a bad question or that you somehow come across badly. Embrace the silence and you will likely be rewarded with a thoughtful response.

Tone of voice. The tone of your voice and your body language can often communicate more than the actual words that you say. You may be totally unconscious about what you've communicated. So, to the degree you can be thoughtful about your tone and what you communicate, remember that you are sending a signal when you ask questions and when you engage in any conversation. The more you are prepared with preplanned questions, the clearer and more confident you are likely to sound.

Dynamics: one-on-one versus two or a small group. Although you may plan to interview one individual or a series of individuals to solicit answers to your questions, it is entirely possible that you may find yourself in a small group. For example, if you have met someone at a networking event and have planned to visit them at their office for a follow-up interview, they may invite someone else into the discussion. If this happens, remember that you need to try and include the additional person in the discussion and responses to your questions. This outcome can be quite positive for you from a learning perspective, but the dynamic of more than a one-on-one discussion will create some differences in terms of the interaction and the information you are able to collect. It is OK to request that you do the interviews separately but be prepared to follow the lead and preference of the SME who you initially approached.

What to share and when. There are several things that you may want to share or be asked to share. First, as with framing, you may be asked to speak a bit about what your objective is, how you are pursuing it, or why it is an issue for you. Some of your respondents may want to know who you've talked to and what they have shared previously. As a result, you should give thought about what you're willing to share and whether or not you are comfortable disclosing details such as names, titles, or other identifying characteristics. If you've interviewed an executive in your organization and they ask you to disclose who else you talked with and what they said, this may put you in an awkward position. If you're concerned about this be prepared with a response that sounds plausible. For example, you can say "I'm talking to a lot of folks and have promised them, just as I promise you, that I will not share their names. In aggregate though, here's what I'm hearing." If you have no concern over revealing names or specifics you can certainly do this; however, it is wise to ask the people you've questioned if it is OK to disclose their assistance.

Summarize and reflect. At or near the end of your conversation, it may be a good idea to synthesize the conversation and make a few statements about what you heard, and, what your interpretation and takeaway is from the conversation. In this way, you're able to learn *and* confirm your learning. You may want to make a statement about what you plan to do next or how they've helped you. In addition to this reflection and summary, always be sure to thank the individual and do try to leave the door open for a follow-up conversation at another point in time.

Notes

1 www.criticalthinking.org/pages/socratic-teaching/606
2 http://thesecondprinciple.com/teaching-essentials/five-basic-types-questions/; www.skillsyouneed.com/ips/question-types.html; www.umich.edu/~elements/probsolv/strategy/cthinking.htm; https://en.wikipedia.org/wiki/Question

Bibliography

Conradie, Y. (2017). The Art of Asking Good Questions. Retrieved: www.mindtools.com/blog/mttalk-ask-good-questions/

Scamen, Z. (2018). The Lost Art of Asking Questions. Available: https://blog.usejournal.com/the-lost-art-of-asking-questions-8f2bf02f27ed

Skills You Need (Retrieved May, 2019). Types of Questions. Available: www.skillsyouneed.com/ips/question-types.html

The Foundation for Critical Thinking (Retrieved May, 2019). Socratic Thinking. Available: www.criticalthinking.org/pages/socratic-teaching/606

University of Michigan (Retrieved May, 2019). The Six Types of Socratic Questions. Available: www.umich.edu/~elements/probsolv/strategy/cthinking.htm

Wikipedia (Retrieved May, 2019). Question. Available: https://en.wikipedia.org/wiki/Question

Wilson, L. O. (Retrieved May, 2019). 5 Basic Types of Questions. Available: http://thesecondprinciple.com/teaching-essentials/five-basic-types-questions/

8   The Art of Observation

When was the last time you watched someone to see how they performed a task? Have you ever watched a *YouTube* video to see how to fix something around your home or apartment? When learning occurs through observing others it is called observational learning. Everyone has learned this way – we observe our parents, teachers, friends, and even people who we don't know. If you watch an athlete take a swing, roll a ball, or take a shot, then try the technique yourself, you are attempting to learn through observation. Sometimes this learning is more subtle and the emulation of an act is less direct or intentional. Learning to walk or eat is more instinctual but often reflects the style of others to whom we are close. Because modeling occurs all the time, we often hear about the concept of someone being a "good role model" or conversely of someone being a "poor role model." In the workplace, we see examples of good and poor role model behavior on a daily basis and hope that the former is more prevalent than the latter. It's commonplace to observe; there is an art to doing it well – and doing it with the intent to develop your behavior proficiency.

When you get a degree or other credential you learn typically by listening to subject matter experts and by consuming deep subject matter. You may memorize information or learn about the issues related to certain topics. You may hear or read about examples or applications of content to real life by discussing case studies or case vignettes. In some instances, you may even see videos with applications or with subject matter experts. For most competencies this is great background and important to know. However, for the bulk of behavioral competencies, this may not be sufficient for developing your proficiency and skill. When you are learning a new skill it often takes technical knowledge, practice, and observation. Chapter 6 discussed ways to practice through the Art of Role Playing and this chapter adds another tool to the self-directed learning approach. Observation helps individuals interpret what they see and, in some cases, emulate what they see. That said, there needs to be a way to structure when, how, where, who, and why you observe for the purpose of skill building.

The Science Behind Observational Learning

There are incredible insights to be gained by watching people and situations.[1] We often go through our day in a bit of a blur; shifting from meeting to meeting or task to task. When we take the time to soak up what we see and think about it, in context, we can make greater sense of what we observe and can use it as a learning tool.[2] Observation itself is easy, but to make it a learning tool we need to be more mindful of the process and practice in our approach to observation. Practicing the art of observation will help you to be less obvious in your observation endeavors and more skillful in extracting useful information.

When observing, you will need to decide if what you're witnessing is a behavior pattern, or, if it is an anomaly. While it is absolutely possible to learn from something you see once, or even that which is an anomaly, it is important to learn from behavior patterns that are displayed regularly – and that you know have the impact you want to achieve. As children, we "modeled" our parents, siblings, teachers, and friends. This is called *social learning* and it occurs by watching the behavior of others. Much of social learning is based on Albert Bandura's social cognition learning theory.[3] In the dissemination of this theory, Bandura outlined four stages and made a distinction between learning and performance. He argued that in order to display learned performance, the observer had to be motivated. The motivation comes from reinforcement that is either external or internal – the underlying point is that there must be reinforcement. The four stages of social learning include:[4]

- Attention – paying attention to what is around you, and in particular the person from whom you want to learn.
- Retention/memory – recognizing a behavior, and remembering it later so it can be pulled out of memory storage for use later.
- Reproduction/initiation – ability to reproduce behavior; this will likely take practice.
- Motivation – must be motivated to use the behavior; usually an incentive or stimulus to reproduce is necessary. This is where reinforcement (or punishment) comes into play.

The application of this model to everyday managerial behavior is witnessed often. Sometimes the influence is quite positive and other times it can have negative effects. For example, the manager who makes it a point to greet his or her staff each day using a name, a positive tone, and an appropriate greeting, may elicit this same behavior in others. This sets the work culture and tone in a positive way. Conversely, the manager who walks silently by staff as they enter a work area, or who mumbles or says something negative may set a poor example and elicit work stress and dissatisfaction. Now, imagine these two contrasting behaviors and the impact they have on other staff (observers). Those who are greeted positively may be more motivated to be positive in response to others and those who are greeted negatively may be similarly disposed to pass on a negative tone, or if not negative, then at least not positive. This form of engagement, or lack of engagement, may be reinforcing future behavior. Of course, behavior is not always this black-and-white, but the point is that behavior of others is often modeled and is certainly influential.

Given this relationship and the clear stages in the process, it is possible to be more analytical and purposeful in using observational learning as a tool to develop managerial proficiency. Each stage offers an opportunity to the learner to be purposeful in their approach.

Attention

Given that some days or events can go by in a blur, or at least not always allowing for reflection due to a focus on the task or meeting at hand, taking the time to focus on what is happening around you in a given situation can lead to the observer noticing important details and behavior. For instance, if every Monday you participate in a team meeting designed to review activities from the previous week and plan for the upcoming week, what do you do, or notice others do, in preparation? Is the meeting routine and your assumption is that everyone will behave in typical fashion – boss kicks off the meeting, staff report out one by one, Terri arrives late, Chad fidgets with his cell phone, and the meeting ends exactly 30 minutes after it starts? Observational learning occurs when you focus beyond the routine. It may begin by noticing what the boss does upon entering the meeting room: are there greetings, are cell phones turned off, is a notepad or a handout in front of the boss? More importantly, what has the boss done to prepare for the meeting? Is there an agenda – are there specific points jotted down about what will be covered? Are the items checked off as the meeting progresses? How does the boss respond to Terri when she arrives late or to Chad who is fidgeting with his phone? What is the impact on the meeting? Is the result distraction, interruption, annoyance? What influence does this reaction have on the meeting? Does the boss take notes; are assignments given; and how was the meeting opened, conducted, and concluded? There are many behavioral cues that can be noticed if one thinks about the environment. In addition, there are emotional cues to notice – do you like or respect your boss and colleagues? How do *you* feel about Terri's tardiness and Chad's fidgeting? All of this influences your attention and hence your learning.

Retention

We all notice many things each day. We may or may not pay attention to all of the details and behaviors. If we want to retain what we've observed so that we can replicate the behaviors of a model or, conversely, ensure that we do not replicate negatively perceived behaviors, we need to have a method for doing so. This can be as simple as saying to yourself "Hm, that's an interesting approach to running a meeting, I'll have to try that the next time I'm in a position of running a meeting." Considering how busy your day may get, ensuring that you retain what you've observed may involve more structure so you can codify the behavior you want to replicate. One way to do this is by writing down the cues and the information you see. This can be accomplished by using a journal (Chapter 9); however, carrying a journal with you throughout the day may not be practical and the environment may not be conducive for writing long narratives. Moreover, your primary attention should be focused on your job.

One possible way is to informally write notes to yourself in the margins of your agenda, type by fingering something into your phone or tablet, or by committing your observations to paper as soon as you are able. Some people like sending themselves an e-mail with notes, so the idea is not lost. A second and more formal structure is to use a worksheet or form to capture the detail that might help you. Having a structure provides an immediate way to organize your thoughts and will likely take less time or attention to create. Worksheet 8.1 provides one sample of what this may look like. The benefit of a template is that it will prompt you to remember information that may be helpful. This worksheet can be used directly, or, you can easily build your own worksheet to suit the needs of your planned observation. With an approach like this there is latitude to make printed copies and carry blank worksheets with you in whatever notebook you use throughout the day, or you can create a soft copy template of the worksheet to use on what-ever devices you regularly carry. A worksheet is a good idea if you are doing a planned observation rather than informally noticing something. The worksheet creates some space for the details to which you should pay attention and also provides structure to help you remember what you've witnessed – and ways in which you can begin to reflect on how you will model the behavior you've witnessed. Example 8.1 illustrates how Chris, our senior manager highlighted in Chapter 2, can apply the observation worksheet for developing her presentation skills.

Initiation

Performing or reproducing the behavior is the next stage. Unlike a child or an athlete who is trying to reproduce a behavior specifically, you may be trying to reproduce an approach or a set of behaviors around a theme or competency. For example, like Chris, if someone is trying to develop presentation skills, they may design a plan to observe a variety of presenters in a range of presentation scenarios. Further, they may need to practice their delivery or presentation in order to rep-licate the behavior they wish to model. In an example like this, the observer may wish to create a dedicated template for observing to prompt them to focus on specific things they want to reproduce.

Motivation

In order for an observer to copy the positive behaviors they have seen; they must be motivated to do so. Clearly, by observing with intent there is a foundation of motivation to develop your skills. Using the example above of developing presen-tation skills, think about the impact of a well-placed cartoon, quotation, or appli-cation. If an audience laughs at cartoons or appears more focused as a result of the use of cartoons then the idea of using cartoons will be reinforced. As a result, the motivation can be both direct motivation for the observer, like receiving feed-back from a boss that their presentation skills need improvement, and indirect by

Worksheet 8.1 Observation Template

Date:	Competency:
Description *of observation/event:*	
Planned *observation or* **ad hoc** *occurrence:*	
What are 3 or more specific things you noticed related to your competency target?	1. 2. 3.
What reflections do you have about what you've observed?	
How will you internalize what you observed?	What will you do (or try) now: What will you stop doing: Who will you follow up with:
Is there anything else unique or remarkable to note about the observation?	

observing others' experience – in this case, witnessing the positive response to a well-placed cartoon. Although you may be motivated, consider creating some sort of reward for yourself for skill development attainment. For example, plan a reward, something personally appealing to you that is a treat, for when you reach a milestone. The milestone can be when you receive praise from your boss for an effective presentation. The reward can be going to your favorite restaurant or something else you feel is a treat.

Now that the stages of social learning are clear we must still address the questions of when, how, where, who, and why you observe for the purpose of building management skills.

Example 8.1 Observation Template – Chris

Date:	Competency: *Presentation skills*
Description of observation/event: *Presentation to senior staff*	

Presenter name: *Thomas G. Executive from Europe in acquiring company*	**Presentation location**: *Main conference room*
Topic: *Doing business abroad; new business initiatives*	**Length:** *2 hours*

Describe 3 or more things about the presenter's style.	1. *Thomas was quite polished and his slides were incredibly sophisticated.* 2. *He was confident and direct and did not want questions until he solicited them from the group.* 3. *It was assumed that we were already familiar with the products and line of business.*
What reflections do you have about what you've observed?	*It's clear that lots of changes are coming; the business is going to change but more than that the polish and approach will be much more formal; in order to be successful, you have to present with conviction and be able to clearly state your point and communicate in a persuasive way.*
Describe 3 or more things about the impact the presenter had on the audience.	1. *He was a bit intimidating but impressive on how smart he was.* 2. *Makes me realize that I will need to be much better at influencing others in the future and that the new company will expect initiative.* 3. *My presentation style will need to be stronger and my assistant will need to be an expert with the presentation software they use.*
How will you internalize what you observed?	What will you do (or try) in your next presentation: *Add charts, graphics, and color to the slides; be prepared with examples and additional evidence.* What will you stop doing in your next presentation: *Need to train myself not to use our company name and to use product names more often.* Who will you follow up with to confirm your new approach to presenting: *Should call a meeting with the members of my team to let them know what data and information to start collecting to be used in future presentations.*
How will you practice or reproduce what you have learned?	*Even though it will be three months before the acquisition is complete, I should start now to change my approach to presenting so that I display more polish and can demonstrate a stronger style; this will also start the change management process with my team.*
What is unique, different, and/or appealing about the presentation (i.e., cartoons, handouts, colors, pictures, etc.)	*The slides looked as though they were professionally done – will need to check on how this was accomplished. I liked the way the company logo appeared on all the slides and how they used the same color scheme in the font to match the logo. The use of few words on the slides was appealing and the use of additional talking points to support the concepts was well done. Humor was absent but I'm not sure if that was due to this being so new.*

Effective Observation

Effective observation can be accomplished by working through a series of questions relating to the competency that you are trying to develop. This includes the who, what/how, where, when, and why. The answers to all these wh-questions may be different for each competency on your priority list.

When

As we know, observation occurs all the time. We are constantly scanning our environment and watching what happens when, who does what, and seeing any number of cues in the environment. At times, while driving a car for example, we are highly attuned to the environment, paying attention to road signs, other cars, pedestrians, and the like. At other times, while a passenger in a car, we are less attuned to the environment because we are not immediately responsible for driving the car safely. Informally, we may learn things every day. We pick up a new phrase to mimic, we see a valuable resource, we are exposed to a new perspective, or any other tidbits both large and small. These incidents occur regularly but are often not preplanned. Observation as a learning technique can be preplanned or ad hoc. When planned, it can be used as a proactive tool to develop proficiency.

When in this instance is not meant to just answer the questions of time, date, time frame in career, or some other time-based event. Included is the question of *when* in a learning journey does it make sense, if at all, to employ observation as a strategy for direct learning. When also refers to: at what point in your day or job or personal time does it make sense to employ a structured observation approach with the objective of developing proficiency in a particular competency? When you have received feedback that you need to improve your presentation skills – the *when* is now. If you, after your own self-assessment, wish to be proactive in developing your presentation skills then the *when* is fit into your prioritization of developing the competencies identified during your initial assessment.

What and How

To learn from observation with an objective to focus on a specific skill or competency you need a structured approach that supports milestones, diversity of input, integration of content, and observations. The *how* in this context does not suggest that informal day-to-day observation and learning should stop or be discounted; it does suggest that a more sophisticated and focused system of observation will lead to learning and, more importantly, skill development. The following are some recommendations by *what* means to accomplish the *how*.

- Create specific objectives (see Worksheet 8.2)
- Create realistic milestones
- Plan how you will balance participation (in a meeting, for example) with your focused observation

- Create an intake observation form to collect data and ideas systematically (see Worksheet 8.1)
- Plan follow-ups with people for other activities, like role play
- Don't observe in isolation – plan several opportunities for observation
- Distinguish between formal and informal observation for developmental purposes

The *how* can be accomplished in many different ways. It will depend on the nature of your job, industry, profession, work environment, country, and organization culture. The fact is that because these things vary, the observer must take charge of the *how* and create the necessary structure to ensure that what is observed will support learning.

Worksheet 8.2 provides a suggestion of an observation schedule and planning approach. By listing the competencies you are focusing on and by thinking through the what, who, when, where, and why, you can be prepared to observe in an organized way. By being systematic you are likely to notice much more than if you were unstructured. Worksheet 8.2 can be used as a regular exercise to help you focus. For example, this worksheet can be completed weekly by looking at your upcoming schedule and noting at which meetings, networking events, planned interactions, and so forth there may be useful opportunities for observation of the skills you are trying to develop. It is also a good way to determine whether or not there are enough organic opportunities to observe or if you will need to seek more specific opportunities to allow for observation of the competencies you wish to develop. This means you may need to seek out specific opportunities where observing the competency you wish to develop is likely to be found. If this is the case, you may need to coordinate this with a boss or someone else who may be able to provide access to the opportunity.

Where

The simple answer is anywhere. The reality, however, is that while observation for learning can occur in any organization, at work or not at work, with coworkers or with friends and family, there are some locations that will be more conducive than others for learning. Consider the possibilities listed in Table 8.1. Can you think of any others that may be available to you?

These are primarily office and professional settings. Keep in mind that valuable observation opportunities can also occur at home, in religious venues, at restaurants, volunteer organizations, and other external events or interactions. When your focus is on self-directed learning and you begin the journey to develop your managerial proficiency, you will likely become more attuned to observational opportunities and will see a range of opportunities that you may not have previously noticed. Worksheet 8.2 can also help you to see patterns and encourage you to think more deeply about where opportunities for observation may be found. Remember, if an opportunity to observe a skill that you need does not present itself – then look for an opportunity outside of your immediate environment.

Worksheet 8.2 Observation Schedule

	Competencies you've identified as a priority: *Use two sheets if necessary*			
	1.	**2.**	**3.**	**4.**
	List competency:	List competency:	List competency:	List competency:
What to observe:				
Who to observe:				
When to observe:				
Where to observe:				
Why will this help:				
Opportunities for observation:				
Notes on completion:				
Notes on practice:				

Why

The *why* question relates not to the *what* but to the *what for.* That is, what is the problem or the reason behind a desire to learn something through observation? Your purpose may be to see the range of how other people approach a particular skill, or, it could be because you are tackling something you've never done before. One way to explore the *why* is to go back to your self-assessment. Couple this with the motivation you have for wanting to develop your managerial proficiency. The key issue will be whether your motivation is from within or if it is externally driven.

Table 8.1 Opportunities for Observation

- Attending a business lunch or dinner
- Attending professional networking events
- Company social gathering
- During an interview – either as the interviewer or interviewee
- During meetings
- During recurring committee meetings
- Impromptu discussion/interaction
- In open spaces compared to closed (for example, office vs. auditorium)
- In the employee kitchen
- Interactions with internal people compared to external people
- Meeting one-on-one with someone
- Meeting with clients or vendors
- Watching employees, in a natural way, interact with one another
- While participating in training either internally or externally
- While training with colleagues

Granted, if a supervisor provides feedback for you to develop a particular competency, the impetus may be both external ("I want to keep my job") and internal ("I want to develop this skill"). Doing something because you're told to do so, without any internal motivation, may make the observation exercise one that is less effective. This is true, of course, for the application of any self-directed learning tool.

Who

It's important to realize that you can learn from anyone, regardless of their level, gender, race, technical expertise, or any other characteristic. Each person or possible target of your observation can be someone from your current environment or someone from past relationships, such as bosses, subordinates, or coworkers. Think broadly about those who you may benefit from observing. In addition to those who you encounter in your business and personal life, you may find that observing people when you are out and about is also insightful. For example, if you are at a business lunch or dinner, you may observe someone you don't know interacting with someone else at a nearby table. Watching an interview, for example, when you have no personal stake in the interaction may allow you to see things that you may not have otherwise noticed. Take the opportunity to observe whenever and wherever possible. Table 8.2 shows a range of possible observation targets. One potential approach is to ask someone if they have any relevant possibilities for you to observe. For example, if you are trying to build your skills at dealing with difficult situations you can ask someone who you know particularly well, if they have a conversation (with the client or vendor) coming up where the discussion may be challenging, if you can be an observer in the room without actively participating in the conversation.

Improving Your Power of Observation: Tips for Success

Observation can be both fun and enlightening. At times it may even be confusing. It is an important self-directed learning tool that is relatively safe, low-cost,

Table 8.2 Sources of Observation

- Board members
- Boss
- Boss's boss
- Boss's boss's boss
- Classmates
- Clients
- Consultants
- Coworkers
- Executives
- Family members
- Friends
- HR leaders
- Icons in your field
- Other managers
- Peers
- Professors, instructors, teachers
- Roommates
- Subject matter experts
- Subordinates
- Vendors

and easy to accomplish once you develop your observational skills. In a world where we are observing all the time, it makes sense to learn from our efforts. Much of observational learning is useful in helping to develop behavioral skills, since behavior is what you are observing. To be useful, we may need to do some advanced learning in order for observation to be effective. For example, if you are developing negotiation skills you may need to have additional learning and knowledge of negotiation tactics or contracts above and beyond the behaviors one displays in an actual negotiation. Approaching this in a purposeful way will allow for greater learning and more effective application.

Observation has many advantages. It is relatively easy to do and is fairly low-cost both in terms of money and time. We can be safe and anonymous – unless you choose otherwise. It is also nonconfrontational in that you can watch behaviors and reactions and then draw your own interpretations and conclusions. You can discuss your reflections, or not, and any observation can be planned in advance or be impromptu. Observation is a learning strategy that is always with you and by practicing observation you have a learning tool that is portable, effective, and lifelong. As you begin to incorporate a strategy of observation into your learning journey there are some pointers that can help you approach this journey more effectively.

Take your time observing. A glance or brief look is not observation. In order to soak in what you are seeing and make sense of the behavior, and reactions to behavior, do not be quick to think you've seen enough. Look for details and consider the reactions of others – which may not occur immediately. Consider the context and any other environmental factors that may be influencing the behaviors you are witnessing.

Reflect. In addition to taking your time and absorbing what you're observing, think through what you've seen. Consider what the motivations may be and contemplate how things may have played out had there been different behaviors. As you reflect, challenge yourself to think about the situation from a different perspective or how you would feel if you were in any of the shoes of those involved.

Do not jump to conclusions. In the same vein as taking your time with the actual observation, do not be too quick to judge what you think you see and assume a conclusion which may or may not be accurate. Reflection can help you avoid a premature conclusion. A follow-up discussion with someone who was in the situation may be warranted to better understand emotions or reactions – and to learn of any conclusions which may not have been evident at the time.

Focus on both verbal and nonverbal cues. In addition to the actual words that are uttered or exchanged, focus also on the tone of voice and other body language cues.[5] Observe things like; eye contact, smiles, frowns, expressions, distance, handshakes, other contact, hand gestures, tone, loudness, and so forth. There is a lot to be learned from verbal and nonverbal cues beyond the spoken content of what is said or exchanged.

Don't be overt. Unless you have asked for permission to observe or let someone know that you are going to observe them for learning purposes, then you may wish to be less than obvious that you are observing and taking notes on what someone says or does. The reason for this is not to hide what you're doing but rather to ensure that what you're witnessing is genuine behavior. If someone knows or senses that they are being watched for a purpose, they may alter their behavior to come across in a specific way. This may or may not support your learning.

Try to look when no one thinks you're watching. Similar to not being overt, you may also want to try and watch an interaction without someone seeing you as part of the situation. For example, if there is an interaction between coworkers or between two senior managers and you happen to be nearby, do not be obvious in your observation. If you are part of the situation, you can't help but be overt in your participation or in someone's awareness of your presence, but you can be more covert in your exercise of observing with a purpose.

Make mental comparisons. Learning may arise from not only what you see but also in noticing differences and considering how effective one scenario was versus another. For example, observing the same person interacting with two different people, either at the same time or in two different settings, and comparing the interactions by noticing word choice, voice tones, body language, and so forth can be enlightening. Comparisons can be of different people in the same scenario or it can be of the same person in different scenarios. Think through what drives behavior and what environmental cues may be at work in addition to personal characteristics. You may also benefit from comparing what you have done or would have done in the same scenario.

Journal your reactions (see Chapter 9). Observation may certainly make you think and you may learn from what you witness. Greater learning will come from reflecting on what you've observed and one effective way to do this is by keeping notes in a journal. Although we may journal about what we observe and find many positive uses for this information, keep in mind that being more structured about your observations can enhance the learning.

Note patterns in people and situations. Looking for patterns is one effective way to determine if there are important trends or formulas to consider. For example, observing how bosses greet staff every morning or how they close out the day can provide insights into their behavior and staff behavior. Looking at how this may differ on a Monday versus a Friday or on a day when there are deadlines or other work stressors can provide valuable insight.

Listen don't just watch. It should go without saying that when you are observing you are also listening to what is being said and how it is said. Turn your attention to what is being said by listening for cues beyond the content.[6] For example, can you tell if someone is asking for input on something when they really do not want the feedback or, conversely, that they want help, but are reluctant to directly request input? Listening in this case means attending to subtle inferences as well as the true meaning of the words.

Engage others. Discuss what you've seen with someone you trust or respect. If you notice something and are not sure it was the right thing to do, try discussing the scenario with someone and asking for their viewpoint or interpretation. This is especially helpful if it is someone who has observed the same thing. To ensure that you don't come across as gossiping, you may want to approach this by suggesting that the discussion be a debrief to confirm what you thought and witnessed.

Practice. Once you see a behavior or approach that you want to copy, you need to practice and try it out yourself. Using the behaviors you've observed and want to acquire will help you to make the behaviors routine and build your capacity in acting the way you think is an improvement over what you've been doing in the past. Practice can be on your own or with others. See Chapter 6 for more insights from role playing. Worksheet 8.2 also prompts you to think about practice.

Make it your own. Modify the words, tone, timing, etc. to suit your personality and needs. Social learning does not mean that you must do something exactly as you've witnessed it. You can pick up a lot of good examples and behaviors by watching someone give a presentation; and when it comes to your turn to give a presentation your style may be more effective by incorporating a combination of what you've observed and what reflects your personality and your manner.

Ask questions. Do not be bashful of following up with the people you've observed. If you're confused by why someone did what they did or why someone reacted as they did, take the time to follow up in a respectful way. "Jim, I noticed that Dan seemed reluctant to accept the strategy you laid out. Why do you think that was the case? I thought the reasoning was sound. Am I missing something?" Asking questions can clarify a situation and may uncover additional information that helps to explain what happened and why. The follow-up does not need to imply that you were purposefully observing and can simply be a result of a natural occurrence.

Notes

1 www.inc.com/justin-bariso/an-fbi-agents-9-ways-to-read-people.html
2 www.verywellmind.com/what-is-observational-learning-2795402
3 www.simplypsychology.org/bandura.html
4 www.verywellmind.com/social-learning-theory-2795074
5 www.mind-expanding-techniques.net/mindpower/people-observation-html/
6 www.psychologytoday.com/us/blog/emotional-freedom/201402/three-techniques-read-people

Bibliography

Bariso, J. (2015). An FBI Agent Shares 9 Secrets to Reading People. *Inc.* Available: www.inc.com/justin-bariso/an-fbi-agents-9-ways-to-read-people.html

Cherry, K. (2019). How Social Learning Theory Works. *Very Well Mind.* Available: www.verywellmind.com/social-learning-theory-2795074

Cherry, K. (2019). How Observational Learning Affects Behavior. *Very Well Mind.* Available: www.verywellmind.com/what-is-observational-learning-2795402

McLeod, S. (2016). Bandura – Social Learning Theory. *Simply Psychology.* Available: www.simplypsychology.org/bandura.html

Orloff, J. (2014). Three Techniques to Read People. *Psychology Today.* Available: www.psychologytoday.com/us/blog/emotional-freedom/201402/three-techniques-read-people

Socrates. (2011). People Observation: Improve Your Social Skills. *Mind Expanding Techniques.* Available: www.mind-expanding-techniques.net/mindpower/people-observation-html/

9   The Art of Journaling

How long ago did you last take notes on something you saw or thought about for your development? Do you actively keep a personal journal? Some people keep a movie, productivity, finance, dream, or diet journal whereas others never give a single thought to keeping a journal. Journaling is the process of recording thoughts and ideas in a single place such as a diary, logbook, notebook, or another repository – either in written form or electronically. Regardless of where or how you accomplish journaling, it is an exercise in reflection and observation. Reflection is the process of writing down, to examine and think through things you've seen or experienced to create clarity and understanding of your own and others' behavior.[1] It's easy to fall into the trap of thinking that keeping a journal is something teenagers do or something that is assigned in a college class. On the contrary, reflection can help to develop meaning and perspective on both competencies and on the proficiency you have or that you see in others. Indeed, some studies have shown that people who journal are healthier – both mentally and physically.[2]

Why Journal

People have journaled since, well, since people have been writing. There are many reasons why people journal – or should journal. There are also many reasons people give for why they can't or don't choose to journal. Table 9.1 provides some insight as to why people do and don't journal. As you can see, the pros and cons vary widely from professional to personal and even include biases that may or may not be well-founded. Journaling for personal pleasure and insight is not something that needs to be regimented. It is up to the journal writer whether you make entries daily, weekly, or on no specific schedule at all. Journaling for development and learning does not need to be rule-based but will be far more effective if there are some parameters around which you approach journaling. A key advantage of journaling is that it promotes systematic thinking by helping the writer to organize and sort through ideas, issues, or concerns. A primary reason why journaling can be useful is that it requires reflection and introspection. While you may write down facts and actual things you see or hear, a journal needs to include thought, rumination, speculation, impressions, and other independent "brain" work. This is what drives the learning process and allows you to develop new behaviors or leave some practices behind.

Table 9.1 Reasons People Do and Don't Journal

Reasons Given for Journaling[3]	Reasons Given for Not Journaling[4]
• Capture ideas • Chronicle progress on something • Create a connection to goals, emotions, values • Explore thoughts • Facilitate personal growth • Help solve problems • Improve insight and understanding • Improve mental clarity • Improve organizational skills • Improve writing • Keep track of decisions both personal and professional • Keep track of things (e.g., spending, weight loss, hours worked) • Plan for the future • Record interactions with people • Record what works and what doesn't work • Reflection and self-awareness • Self-improvement • To de-stress • Track critical incidents or details (after an accident, for example) • Track personal development • Track success	• Don't have the inclination • Don't have the time • Don't know where to start • Don't see what will be gained by journaling • Don't think that journaling will really help me • Handwriting is terrible • I'd be afraid I wasn't doing it right • It's too hard to get into the habit of journaling • Just don't see the point • My life is just not that interesting • Not a good writer • Spelling is abysmal • There's no immediate gratification • Worry someone will find journal and read it • Worry that if it's sporadic it won't be helpful • Just doesn't appeal to me • Only women keep journals • Only people who are insecure keep journals

In addition to facilitating learning and systematic thinking, journaling can also help to; identify learning needs, deal with frustrations, look for patterns in your behavior, set goals, and congratulate yourself on something you feel positive about that may not have been noticed by others.[5] Developing management proficiency happens when we learn, change our behavior, understand something new, gain a more in-depth perspective, and can think through others' conduct relative to your behavior. There are many benefits to journaling. In addition to the physical and psychological benefits, journaling provides a way to help you solve problems and do so in a creative way. The problem can be an issue that has surfaced in either your work or personal life, or it can be a skill that you need but have not developed to the degree necessary.

How to Journal

To start the journaling process, you need awareness. In the current application, awareness begins at the self-assessment stage, where the competencies to be developed are identified. Once there is awareness of an issue, observation and reflection can occur. Being aware and recording what is seen or heard is only the first step. Examining and analyzing is an integral part of reflection. To be a useful learning tool, the journal must include speculation or thoughts on the motivations behind the behaviors, the delivery, and the impact of the behaviors. Opinion is fine, but it should be backed up by evidence that may be found in the response and the behavior of others. For example, if you spend a day with a colleague or boss out of the office visiting clients and a skill you wish to develop is your *interpersonal effectiveness*, then your journaling may include examples of what your colleague did in various interpersonal situations throughout the day. How did she greet others? How did she treat people such as receptionists, servers, or others who are not the direct client? How did she listen? What tone did she use at various times? What nonverbal cues did she give? How did others react to her? And so on. Make note also of your behavior, tone, delivery, and so forth in the same situations. Calling on your power of observation (Chapter 8), journaling is a process that you manage and initiate to help make sense of what you've noticed.

As the journaling on this day out of the office with your boss or colleague takes shape, focus not on the business outcome per se but reflect on the single focus of interpersonal effectiveness both positive and, if present, the negative. Analyze the behaviors in the interpersonal interactions throughout the day. Evaluate both your colleague's behavior and your own. Be critical in a constructive way as you reflect and analyze. This will increase your self-awareness, and over time, in your journaling, you may see patterns emerge.[6] Better still, you may develop a new perspective and begin to try new or different behaviors. Journaling can help to translate what you think into a modified behavioral approach that is ultimately more effective. The outcome of journaling is that it will spark clearer thinking and should result in better learning. Note that you do not necessarily need to carry around your journal or direct your attention away from client meetings – but you can be mindful of these things and make your journal entries at the end of the day when you have sufficient time to reflect with clarity.

When preparing to journal with a special learning objective in mind, it is helpful to have a competency in mind upon which to reflect and to have some structure or guidelines to follow in collecting thoughts on what you've heard or witnessed. A journal should be more free-flowing; so, rather than having to use a worksheet or something that is too confining, keep in mind a broad set of questions. If you have observed something, consider:

- What was the event: provide some description?
- Who was involved: names, roles, relationship to you, and others?
- What have you learned: to do or not to do?
- What motivations existed?
- How did you feel either as part of the situation or as a witness: positive, negative, energized, concerned, proud, etc.?
- What would you have done the same or differently and why: reflect on self-awareness of your behaviors?
- What can I, or should I, try doing differently in the future to be more effective?
- Should I follow up with anyone to gain clarity on what happened?
- Note relevant facts such as date, time, location, etc.

Worksheet 9.1 Getting into the Swing of Journaling

<u>Instructions</u>: This exercise can be repeated multiple times and you can add your own observations or additional questions.

Prompt 1: *Think about the last meeting you attended, was there anything that either frustrated you or excited you? Write down what it was and why you felt the way you did.*
Prompt 2: *Think about the next meeting you are scheduled to attend, are you looking forward to it or are you dreading it? Write down what you look forward to or dread and why you feel the way you do.*
Prompt 3: *Think about your best friend at work (i.e., the person you spend the most time with or whose company you enjoy the most). What is their best professional quality and what is their best personal quality? If you had to give this person feedback on something to improve, what would it be and why?*
Prompt 4: *Think about your own behavior at work, what is one thing that you think you need to work on and improve? What would your boss say about this behavior? What would a subordinate or colleague say about this behavior?*

Are You a Journal Novice?

If you have little or no experience with journaling, it may seem like a daunting or uncomfortable task. If so, Worksheet 9.1 may help you to practice journaling or come to enjoy the activity. Getting into the mode of reflecting and writing down your feelings can be awkward. However, after you do this exercise a few times, you may find that it is easier and more comfortable to journal. When you journal, you can write about anything you wish. The point, however, is to write about something that you've thought about or that you will benefit from thinking about more deeply. It doesn't matter if you write a lot or a little, if you use complete sentences or not, and if you are always positive or negative. What matters is whether or not you learn from the activity. Learning can be in the form of picking up a new skill or behavior, gaining insight or wisdom about something, obtaining new knowledge, or understanding something you had previously not thought about or understood. Journaling can be a more subtle form of learning; however, it can lead to other self-directed learning tools. Journaling can spark the need or desire to network, role play, develop questions, and point to additional observation that may be helpful.

Observation Versus Reflection

The example questions presented earlier are a combination of journaling as an observer and as a participant of an event or sequence of events. It can also turn into an exercise of your reflection where the journal reflects on client interactions in general. In this latter application, reflection may include comparisons of how people, not just a boss or colleague, interact with others. And it can be an analysis of the reactions of clients (receptionists, servers, etc.) to different styles. The point is that while a specific observation may spark an idea for journaling, it can also be a general reflection on the components of the competency you wish to develop. This list of questions, rather than being directed at someone else, as in preparation for networking or questioning with a purpose, are for you to use to help you reflect. Reflecting on questions like this is something you can do either before or after (or both) you engage in any other learning tools to assist you with skill development. In this way, journaling can help you prepare for other interactions.

If you haven't observed something specific and are thinking through a critical competency, journaling can help prepare you to think about the competency and understand multiple aspects of the skill. For example, if the competency is *feedback* – both giving and receiving – consider developing a list of questions or issues and then free form your responses. Your journal entries can include everything from random ideas to both simple and complex thoughts[7] – for example, here are some questions to ponder in a journal to go along with the competency of feedback:

- When is it important for people to receive feedback?
- How should you respond if/when people request feedback?
- Should I ask for feedback?
- What are the barriers for people receiving feedback?
- Why is feedback necessary?
- Do people always appreciate and respond well to feedback?
- What should you do if someone gets emotional from the feedback you deliver?
- How is it best to respond when someone gives you unsolicited feedback?
- What are the things that can make giving feedback easier?
- How do you deliver constructive versus positive feedback differently?
- How can feedback be two-way communication rather than one-way communication?
- What if the person receiving the feedback doesn't change their behavior?

Journaling is a judgment-free zone,[8] and getting your ideas down on paper can help you lay out your thoughts and come up with fresh ideas. This can lead to more questions – or greater clarity. Either way, it is beneficial.

Creating a Journal

Journals can be quite versatile, or, if preferred you can create several different journals each with a different focus.[9] For example, create a journal or a section in your journal for a particular topic, competency, or a specific recurring meeting. A journal is separate from taking notes at meetings or for keeping track of assignments or essential information related to your job or organization. Notetaking can be valuable and, indeed, necessary for keeping track of priorities and information needed to be successful. Journaling, on the other hand, can be useful in developing skills and for internalizing a behavioral understanding of situations. For instance, you may wish to keep a separate journal for each of the competencies you identified in your self-assessment. Alternatively, you can create different sections in a single journal. Make sure you have plenty of space and that the format is conducive to what you want to do.

How to Get Started

Because journaling is a little less structured than the previous learning tools described, there is perhaps less need for a formal template to follow. With a journal, there may not be a formal start or definitive conclusion. To help you organize your thoughts it may be helpful to at least start by establishing your objective, followed by defining what opportunities may exist and including some indication of how you will follow up.

There are a few potential points to write about in a journal. Some journals will be more structured than others and some may focus on a particular skill while others may be broader.

- *Objective*: Start by stating your intention – what do you need to learn? What is the motivation? What, if any, parameters exist – is there a specific time frame or event, etc.?
- *Opportunities*: What opportunities exist associated with your job organization, which might provide an occasion for you to observe or from which to learn? What opportunities exist outside your organization – such as with volunteer roles or personal clubs/interactions?
- *Follow-up*: How will you follow up with what you've learned or observed? How will you apply what you learn and reflect upon your journal entries?

The idea behind journaling in this manner is that you keep all your questions, observations, and notes in one place. Over time, a picture will emerge in which you can put all your learning together. This can begin to influence your behavior and can also direct you to additional learning or practice needs. Grouping your entries by competency area is a great way to stay organized. At some point, you need to reflect on all your thoughts and reflections so that you can take action in terms of your new knowledge, skill, and ability concerning the competency you've tried to develop.

An Example

If *negotiation* skill development is a goal you've identified as a priority but something with which you have little direct experience, an excellent way to start understanding this competency may be in journaling. Starting with some initial and independent research or reading on the subject will be helpful in first knowing what to look for and establishing parameters around what you want to learn or be able to do. Taking notes in your journal on this research can help you internalize the information. Negotiation, for example, can include anything from asking for more time to complete an assignment to negotiating with a supplier on a price, to bargaining with a union. Every scenario, from the simple to the sophisticated, can be important, or emotional, or difficult, or varied in length – the characteristics of a scenario can vary widely. The point is that having a strategy and the right behavioral approach can be the difference between a successful interaction and one which ends with one or both parties disappointed with the outcome. In this example, the journal exercise is all about the topic and may or may not be specifically about an observation of an event or sequence of events. As a result, your approach will be different. Example 9.1 illustrates how Nick, our individual contributor, may prepare himself for management roles in the future. He knows that negotiation will be a skill he needs. He may start by capturing some basic research on the topic and may follow up with entries that both plan ahead and reflect on what he's experienced.

Example 9.1: Journal Entries by Nick

Objective: learn as much as I can about negotiation, observe negotiations in action, and ultimately begin to negotiate on my own.

Entry: 4/22 – Watched Sam negotiate with Danielle about more time to complete the board report due next week; he made a compelling argument and had prepared a list of reasons why more time was needed and how they could extend the deadline and still meet the timeline for preparation in advance of the quarterly meeting.

• Follow up with Sam to ask how he developed this strategy

Entry: 4/24 – Have just been invited to attend a meeting with one of our suppliers; the contract is up for renewal, and my boss thinks this is an excellent learning opportunity for me.

- To prepare, I should familiarize myself with the existing contract, talk with Marty, Sara, and Logan about any concerns they have with the current contract and what they want to see changed if anything.
- Prepare a list of things to look for in the meeting – both behavioral and content.
- Set up a meeting with the boss <u>now</u>, to take place the day after the supplier meeting to do a debrief.
- Ask the boss if it is a good idea for us to chat about the supplier meeting in advance and what his expectations are for my role in the meeting and subsequent negotiation.
- I'm excited! This is a cool opportunity.

<u>Entry</u>: 4/27 – Attended a golf outing today with some friends from my MBA program. Great fun. Learned that Nigel is now working for a multinational organization and has had some interesting dealings and partnerships with companies outside the US.

- Research Nigel's company to understand better what they do and then invite Nigel to lunch one day to talk about differences in approach to negotiations by the different business units across the organization. Is negotiation for more straightforward issues the same or different across cultures? What changes when the negotiation is on a more complex issue?

<u>Entry</u>: 5/3 – Attended the supplier meeting today with my boss. The exchange was fascinating.

- The contract is not up for another month, but both sides were positioning for advantage!
- Supplier seems a little worried. They didn't <u>say</u> this but I kept seeing sideways glances at one another, and they were trying to please my boss.
- They were bending over backward to show how accommodating they are – one of them even sent an e-mail to their HQ to address an issue while his colleague was continuing.
- My boss was a lot more reserved than usual; seemed to be positioning for pushback.
- I heard some problems that came up in my discussions with Marty and Sara, but the things Logan flagged were not even mentioned. I wonder why?
- The supplier left with a pretty long "to do" list. I wonder why they had not addressed these issues sooner? Did they know about them?
- Really glad I scheduled a meeting with the boss for tomorrow! Lots to discuss and learn. This whole process is fascinating. Reminds me a

little about some of the cases in my management class last year – and I thought they were exaggerating!

- I'm glad I was just there to listen. I have a lot to learn about all the posturing. I am surprised that this was less about the product and more about customer service – and we didn't even discuss price yet! I wonder who their competitors are?

Journaling Beyond Your Competency Priorities

Another option in addition to journaling in general or observation brainstorming with yourself about a competency is to engage with others in a planned exercise. Knowing what you think is important, but it may be even more enlightening if you discuss your ideas or observations with someone else. Selecting the right partner is important, and finding someone who you trust and who may benefit from the exercise is also essential. Worksheet 9.2 outlines a journal strategy that is employed by at least two people with the result of either sharing your journal entries, discussing them, or both. This exercise is more structured and the reason is that there needs to be some basis for comparison or discussion. Although journaling tends to be a solitary activity, it can be expanded in this way to help facilitate a discussion and the sharing of information and perspectives.

Using Nick's example scenario, this worksheet could be employed by Nick and either Logan, Sara, or Marty, whoever may have also attended the meeting. Nick and one (or more) of them could agree in advance to do the exercise or Nick could request the exercise afterward with one of them as a way to debrief from the meeting. If he is comfortable doing so, Nick can also do the exercise with his boss.

Improving Your Journaling Approach: Tips for Success

Although journaling does not need to be regimented, there are many factors to keep in mind that will make this learning tool even more useful. Whether you journal every day, every week, or with no particular schedule, journaling can provide you with a great reference for future use. Journaling may not work for everyone, but it is a powerful tool for learning. It is relatively easy to journal and low-cost as well. The most significant investment is the time and commitment it takes to consistently journal and review what you've committed to paper for learning. A journal can be a great resource and reference tool for the future and may be useful for developing future competencies as well. Because a journal is primarily for you alone, it can be a very safe way to think through your observations and learnings without worrying about what others might think, say, or do. Over time, a journal can be quite insightful. And because a journal is done on your own, it is less likely that there will be time issues or time constraints. A final advantage of a journal is that it is portable and can easily accompany you to meetings, business trips, and other work-related or personal activities. This makes the tool flexible

Worksheet 9.2 Partner Journal

Instructions: Select an event and/or a person and competency; partner with a colleague who is interested in the same competency. Define the time frame and parameters (could be a meeting, a day, or something else) and at the end of the exercise discuss your reflections and observations with your partner.

Competency:	Partner:	Date:
Describe the focus in more detail – what is the objective?		
How long will the journal period last?		
What are the parameters (e.g., internal vs. external focus; managers vs. individual contributors, discussion at end or share journal entries; specific meeting, etc.)?		
Observation:	*Observation:*	
Observation:	*Observation:*	
Observation:	*Observation:*	
Observation:	*Observation:*	
Debrief and discussion: • *Did you see/hear the same thing?* • *Was your interpretation the same?* • *Were you accurate about yourself/others?* • *Are outcomes what you expected?* • *What was your focus compared to partner?* • *What observations were unique to each?* • *Did you repeat the same examples?* • *Other questions:*	*Notes:*	

Option: Rather than seeking a partner in advance, after an event, or during a one-on-one conversation with someone you trust, explore their observations, share some of your own, and discuss the reflection and learnings from others.

and easy to maintain. Journaling may seem like a lot of work, but the benefits outweigh the time and effort.

Select a good spot or time to journal. Journaling should be done in a place where you feel comfortable and safe. It should also be done at a time when you can think clearly and have enough time to finish your reflection without having to stop in mid-thought. Some may find journaling in the same place regularly to be helpful; others may prefer variety.

Establish clear objectives. At the start of a journaling episode when focusing on a particular competency, it is a good idea to articulate what you hope to accomplish. Stating the competency is necessary but, as discussed earlier, fleshing out what you want to achieve and breaking down your competency needs to subareas will help you to hone in on what will be most helpful and will facilitate learning. Objectives can have a goal in mind, such as an event or point in time, in addition to the competency.

Reflect often – at least three or four times a week, even daily. Reflection should be continuous rather than sporadic, especially when you are focusing on developing a specific competency. It's much easier to think clearly and develop conclusions and behaviors about a competency when you are thoughtful and continuous regularly. That said, the amount and timing are up to the journal writer. If sporadic is all you can do, keep going rather than abandoning the effort.

Be honest and open – no one needs to see this but you. If your reflection leads you to question how you've been doing something or that the person or situation you observed was negative, follow through and put down candid viewpoints. If your behavior is going to improve or change, then you need to be frank with yourself.

Review what you've written for more significant learning. Writing things down will help you to internalize the ideas, and reviewing them will allow for greater reflection. Besides, as you add more to the journal, studying from the beginning will enable you to build on the ideas and put together a more thorough perspective.

Variety – reflect on various people, scenarios, and issues – around your theme. Use as many different opportunities as possible to offer the broadest possible understanding. If you are looking to enhance your leadership perspective, consider leaders at all levels, backgrounds, and varying characteristics to think through and see themes and different applications. The greater the variety of your reflections, the more likely you are to make comparisons and see distinctions in good versus poor versus superior behavior.

Be evaluative and judgmental – even if you change your perspective over time. If something strikes you as odd, wrong, or out of place, do not hesitate to put this in your journal. Later observations may have you change your mind, but the process of being evaluative and stating an opinion will be helpful from a learning perspective. This means that you need to be flexible and open to evolving your thinking – and in making sense of what you question or dislike.

Don't be afraid to ask questions or to follow up. Asking questions for clarification or further understanding can be helpful. If an idea strikes you about how you think you can evolve your managerial competency and behave differently in the future, you may benefit by talking with someone to confirm, clarify, or deny an idea. It's not necessary to tell someone that the question is based on your journaling – people ask questions all the time.

Select the right journal for your style. Make sure that you're comfortable with what you use and that it's easy – if you like writing in a notebook make sure this is practical and that you'll keep it up. A journal does not need to be fancy or high tech – it needs to be something that fits your personality and style. It should not, however, be on scraps of paper or in dispersed notebooks or pads. How much organization inside the journal is up to you but a single journal, or multiple if you choose to separate the journal by competency, should be used.

Be organized. Create sections or use different notebooks or electronic files for different competencies. The journal does not need to be rule-based or even neat. It can have things crossed out, erased, underlined, highlighted, etc. It should be prepared in such a way that you can pull together your thoughts about a competency rather quickly.

Only share what you're comfortable sharing. The journal is for you. If you choose to share with someone else that's fine but don't share just because you're asked – share if you think it will help you to learn by discussing an issue with someone else. It is also possible to share your ideas with someone without sharing an actual written journal entry. This is totally up to you.

Do not box yourself into a corner. Don't be afraid to change your mind or evolve your thinking over time – journaling should help you get or stay "unstuck" rather than box yourself into a conclusion that may be premature or even wrong. If someone offers an observation or opinion about your behavior or skill, actively consider what is said and reflect in your journal, but don't let this box you in either.

Stay focused. It may be tempting to stray from one competency to another or into solving a problem or ruminating about a troubling new situation. Stay focused, at least in the journal, on the competency you are trying to develop. Going back over your reflections when they are bouncing around will not help draw conclusions and be developmental. If you find yourself distracted or wish to journal about a problem or just journal about something else, make sure it is done elsewhere in the journal so you can maintain focus on your learning goal.

Date your entries. Dating your entries will help to provide context, and you may also be able to go back and look at your calendar or schedule at a later date to determine if any external factors had an influence on what you were thinking at the time. Being sick, having a significant deliverable, getting a new boss or coworker, can all have an impact on your reflections and behavior – and with others as well. It will also help you to see if you've been consistent or random in making entries.

Don't worry about spelling or grammar. On occasion, our minds work faster than our fingers or pens. If you are in the zone with your writing, don't worry if you have made a grammatical error or misspelled something. If you want to go back later and correct something you can always do so, but don't interrupt your writing flow while making entries. Unlike professional writing, a journal does not need to be free from these technical errors.

Experiment. Be creative. Write a letter, create a dialogue, compose an e-mail, write an elevator pitch about one of your competency objectives, etc. A journal can be a place to explore and practice. Try out different phrases or think creatively in a way that will help you to learn and internalize what you have seen, thought, or heard.

Plan. Look at your schedule for the day or week ahead; think about opportunities that may prove fruitful for observation or reflection. This may allow you to bring your journal with you if the opportunity is right. Also, plan the times when you will journal. If you are able, block 30 minutes on your schedule or plan a time each day when you know you can consistently make journal entries, this will help you keep the momentum in and enhance your learning.

Be spontaneous. Planning is essential so that you regularly focus on journaling when you are trying to develop a competency; however, allow yourself to stop at the spur of the moment if you have a reflection that you think might be important in your development journey. There are times when you may notice something important and, rather than losing the thought, try to capture it at the moment.

Consider dictation. If your handwriting is messy or you're not used to writing a lot, consider putting your journal in an electronic file and using dictation. Most smartphones and tablets have this feature, and it may work better for you to dictate rather than write longhand for your entries. This won't work for all people, but it is an option to consider.

Notes

1 www.futurelearn.com/courses/enhancing-learning-and-teaching/0/steps/26451
2 www.mic.com/articles/110662/science-shows-something-surprising-about-people-who-still-journal
3 List was developed by reading many sources, including: https://medium.com/the-mission/10-reasons-to-keep-a-journal-b667d7a8374b; www.lifehack.org/articles/communication/journal-writing-5-smart-reasons-why-you-should-start-doing-today.html; www.huffpost.com/entry/12-reasons-to-keep-a-jour_b_4774745; www.forbes.com/sites/nomanazish/2017/12/29/five-legit-reasons-to-keep-a-journal-in-2018/#5db78d355e18
4 List was developed by reading many sources, including: www.befreeproject.com/befreeproject/10-common-excuses-why-people-dont-journal; www.linkedin.com/pulse/3-reasons-people-hate-journaling-joan-gagnon/
5 www.lifehack.org/articles/lifestyle/reasons-why-you-should-keep-journal.html
6 www.psychologies.co.uk/five-reasons-why-you-should-keep-journal
7 www.inc.com/jessica-stillman/never-been-able-to-keep-a-journal-before-this-is-journal-format-for-you.html

8 www.lifehack.org/articles/lifestyle/reasons-why-you-should-keep-journal.html
9 https://mindbodynetwork.com/article/various-types-of-journals-and-their-use

Bibliography

Future Learning (Retrieved June, 2019). Reflection and Evaluation. Available: www. futurelearn.com/courses/enhancing-learning-and-teaching/0/steps/26451

Grate, R. (2015). Science Shows Something Surprising About People Who Still Journal. *Mic.* Available: www.mic.com/articles/110662/science-shows-something-surprising-about-people-who-still-journal

Psychologies (2018). Five Reasons Why You Should Keep a Journal. Available: www.psychologies.co.uk/five-reasons-why-you-should-keep-journal

Stillman, J. (Retrieved June, 2019). Never Been Able to Keep a Journal Before? This Is the Journal Format for You. *Inc.* Available: www.inc.com/jessica-stillman/never-been-able-to-keep-a-journal-before-this-is-journal-format-for-you.html

Taylor, V. (Retrieved July, 2019). Various Types of Journals and Their Use. *Mind Body Network.* Available: https://mindbodynetwork.com/article/various-types-of-journals-and-their-use

Winter, C. (Retrieved June, 2019). Keeping A Journal Now Will Change Your Life Later. Here's Why. *Lifehack.* Available: www.lifehack.org/articles/lifestyle/reasons-why-you-should-keep-journal.html

Part III

10 The Path Forward

Technical and behavioral skills are essential to do a job well and to advance in an organization. Performing well as a manager requires both technical *and* behavioral skills. Behavioral skills are not only essential; they are often what set us apart and determine how effective you are as a manager. Behavioral skills also have a critical impact on how easy or difficult your job as a people manager is to perform. Most of the competencies identified in Table 2.1 are behavioral or at least highly influenced by behavior. Feeling more at ease and being more effective with these managerial behaviors provides greater satisfaction to both you and your staff. It, therefore, makes sense for managers to focus on development so that you continuously build and maintain your behavior competencies.

As we have seen throughout the book, learning can occur anytime, anywhere. Self-directed learners are in charge of their learning and do so autonomously. Capitalizing on this and being self-directed in our approach enhances learning. The self-directed learning tools described in this book provide an easy and readily available set of tools to stay on track with learning and help to structure the opportunities that are all around us. Self-directed learning allows us to be responsive to our needs *and* to challenge ourselves.

We focused on doing self-assessments and identifying the competencies we need to focus on now and in the future. Although we identify priorities for our learning and commit to developing specific skills, there will always be times when something unexpected occurs or when we find ourselves with a problem or challenge to address. Also, we may see, hear, or experience something that becomes a learning moment even if it doesn't relate to something on our priority list. A self-directed learning mindset shows us that we can take advantage of these opportunities.

Self-directed Learning Mindset

A mindset is a grouping of attitudes toward something. It is a reflection of a viewpoint and can range from loosely held to firmly held beliefs and actions. A mindset can be held by individuals or by groups. You've probably heard people described as having either a fixed or growth mindset about something. The point is that when someone has a "mindset" about something, it means they have a particular

Figure 10.1 Self-directed Learning Mindset

focus. The path forward for managers reading this book is to have a self-directed learning mindset. This does not mean that all your learning must only come from internally motivated activities, nor does it mean that valuable learning can't come from external sources. It does mean that self-directed learning can be a way to achieve success, not only continuous learning. Ongoing professional development will ensure career and personal success. Continuous learning through self-directed learning can lead to job enrichment and job enlargement and can help with job searches, personal growth, and stronger leadership capabilities. Figure 10.1 depicts the many benefits associated with a self-directed learning mindset.

To have a self-directed learning mindset, you need to know who you are, create a plan, manage your time, and adapt as necessary to changes in your needs as a manager.

Learning Moments

Developing competencies that we know we need today or will need in the future is the crux of this book. That said, we often encounter learning moments in the course of a day, a week, a particular project, an event, or some other context. The self-directed learning mindset and skills you have learned in this book can be widely applied and used in many beneficial ways. We know from social learning theory that we observe and learn things all the time. We know from adult learning theory that working adults are self-motivated and learn by doing. Self-directed learning is a skill, and using self-directing learning is a choice. The path forward for those with self-directed learning skills offers unlimited possibilities. Learning moments can occur in both expected and unexpected ways. Although a focus on competencies has been emphasized in this book, you may find many more opportunities to apply your self-directed learning mindset. One thing that a self-directed learning focus has shown us is that the more structured or thoughtful we are, the more likely we are to learn and then be able to apply the skill or behavior elsewhere. Worksheet 10.1 provides a mechanism for capturing important and potentially impactful learning moments. This template can be used to capture the essence of what you see or hear and as a way to extrapolate and apply the ideas and learning. It also provides a way to grab further opportunity by engaging you to think about how you will follow up and implement your behavior or thought.

Worksheet 10.2 is similar, but the focus is on a problem or challenge that you may encounter. As managers, we are often faced with situations that are unexpected or unplanned. A workplace romance that becomes disruptive, an employee who slips from being a high performer to being tardy and low producing, and a shift in leadership, can each create a set of complex circumstances that may test even your most robust competencies. When this happens, you can use all your self-directed learning skills to help you meet and address the challenges more effectively. Situations like these often involve many competencies and require a sequence of behaviors that are compounded and interwoven. Problems like these do not call for just one or two skills to be displayed; they call for management judgment and for many competencies to be demonstrated accurately and successfully. Worksheet 10.2 can be used to help you sort through which behaviors and behavioral approaches you should consider in tackling the challenge or problem. Following up with role plays, observations, journaling, or questioning strategies can help even more.

Opportunities for Learning Are Everywhere

Degrees and credentials are more accessible to obtain than ever before. Online education is widely available and reachable. Certificates, certifications, micro-credentials, and training of all types can be readily found. While cost and easy access may differ, it is still a safe assumption that a focus on learning and development has created more opportunities for managers than previously. Whether or not an organization financially supports your efforts varies widely. Rather than waiting for an organization to offer the opportunity for professional development, or paying for it yourself, a self-directed learning approach provides the learner with boundless opportunities that are customizable to your needs as they exist today and as they evolve tomorrow. Improved management competency can be the difference between:

- Doing a job sufficiently and excelling at the position
- Feeling comfortable and feeling uncomfortable in your role
- Having a positive impact on an organization's bottom line and not having this result
- Getting your next promotion or job offer or not getting the offer

The Path Forward

As you continue to hone your self-directed learning mindset, keep the following things in mind:

Worksheet 10.1 Learning Moments

Describe the learning moment:	
Where: (learning moment occurred)	**Date:**
Circumstance: (was it a meeting, event, chance encounter)	
Context: (who was present or observing)	
Your role: (participant, observer, target, etc.)	

<table>
<tr><td colspan="2" align="center">What you learned:</td></tr>
<tr><td colspan="2">Behavioral learning:</td></tr>
<tr><td colspan="2">Technical learning:</td></tr>
<tr><td colspan="2">New idea:</td></tr>
<tr><td colspan="2" align="center">Follow-up</td></tr>
<tr><td colspan="2">Next steps for reinforcing learning:</td></tr>
<tr><td colspan="2">Seek out someone from learning moment? Who:</td></tr>
<tr><td colspan="2">Questions you have:</td></tr>
<tr><td colspan="2">What else might you learn:</td></tr>
</table>

Instructions: Learning can occur anytime, anywhere. Identifying that learning can help to solidify a new behavior or idea for future use. It can be as simple as a phrase or approach to something more complex such as an effective way to stop a conflict or a method for analytical thinking.

Worksheet 10.2 Problem or Challenge

Describe the problem or challenge:
Circumstance and context: (be as detailed as possible about the issue and the people involved)
Your role: (as a manager, peer, coworker, client, vendor, etc.)
<center>**What you need to be able to do to deal with challenge**:</center>
Behavioral performance:
Technical performance:
Outcome you seek:
<center>**How to approach**</center>
Steps to take:
Who to engage:
How to practice:
Concerns you have:
What self-directed learning tools can be useful to prepare:
Follow-up: What happened

Have a clear vision: or idea in your mind of yourself and your career aspirations. A clear vision helps you pursue the professional development that you need and to assess where you are and where you need to be in the future. A clear vision will allow a self-directed mindset to carry you to new learning opportunities.

Set definitive goals: for the competencies you want to focus on and for the learning priorities it will take to help you reach your vision. Goal setting helps with both specific activities and in setting career and personal milestones. Turn your goals into plans and schedules, so the execution is seamless.

Apply self-directed learning widely: use the learning tools outlined in this book and create additional tools that work for you and in whatever situations you may face. Go beyond the 50 competencies defined in this book and identify others that may be relevant to your business or industry. Becoming a self-directed learner is like learning how to fish – once you have the skill you can tackle any variety, or in this case, any competency. Self-directed learning is a skill – and using it is a choice.

Developing management proficiency is a choice. How you develop your competencies is also a choice. Take the opportunities that are given to you and create opportunities on your own. You've learned to fish in the pond of professional development through self-directed learning – go ahead, have a feast!

Appendix: Case Illustration

This illustration takes one manager, Ben, through both a learning journey and a career development process. Ben has been given the option for a career-changing opportunity, and he will use a self-directed approach to help him think through the opportunity and address what he needs to do to be successful.

Ben is a manager at Newton Products Incorporated (NPI). He has one direct report. Recently, he was approached by his boss, Joan, and his boss's boss, Stefan, about a new initiative that NPI plans to launch in about 12 months. The new product is currently under development and, for competitive reasons, is closely guarded. However, the organization knows that to be successful, they need to have many things ready from multiple parts of the organization at the same time on the day the product launches. Ben's technical expertise is in software interface, and he's recently attained his certification in Project Management. It is this last point, coupled with the fact that Ben is well-liked and well-respected across the organization that NPI has decided to ask Ben to lead a cross-organization task force with the objective of ensuring that all stakeholders are aware of all critical goals related to the launch, support the development of the product, and are working together to ensure alignment and collaboration.

Ben is excited about the opportunity because he's committed to NPI and interested in advancing his career. He also knows that this will be a stretch for him and, therefore, an incredible learning opportunity. Shortly after the euphoria of being offered this opportunity wears off, Ben realizes that he's nervous, in fact, terrified that he doesn't have the knowledge, skills, or abilities to be successful. The meeting with the two bosses took place on a Thursday, and they are expecting a response from Ben on Monday as to whether or not he will accept the offer of this project assignment. It was presented to him as an option rather than an assignment because NPI knows that this is a huge undertaking and that the task force leader will have a demanding year ahead.

Ben and the Opportunity

On Thursday evening Ben sat down and wrote out a list of questions he wanted to ask the next day so that over the weekend he would have as much information as possible to help him make his final decision. He divided the questions into two categories. In the first category, he had questions for Joan and Stefan about resources, timing, expectations, and the like. The second category of questions were targeted at others throughout the organization to find out how easy or challenging this task force might be – this group of questions was much more challenging to formulate and carry out because Stefan asked him to keep the opportunity to himself until Ben made a final decision and it was announced to the whole organization. Ben understood why he was asked to keep the invitation private but also knew it would make getting initial input more difficult.

Over the weekend, Ben started with a blank journal and his favorite pen and began to think about what needs to be done to create the task force and, more importantly, what needs to happen for the task force to be successful. He was able to collect some useful information on Friday and now has a better sense of what needs to be done. He makes a list of the pros and cons of leading the task force. He makes a list of any barriers he thinks might exist inside the organization in doing something like this – since they haven't done anything like this in the recent past. Finally, he makes a list of the experience and skills he has to accomplish everything as well as a list of the skills he thinks he lacks or with which he doesn't have much experience. Ben is a smart and ambitious fellow, but he's also a pragmatist and hard working. He knows he has some learning to do to be prepared for this undertaking. He blue skies a list of other issues, concerns, opportunities, and possibilities.

Self-directed Learning and Self-assessment

Ben has always been self-motivated, curious, and willing to explore areas that he knows little about. Over his three years as a manager and eight years since he obtained his degree in Information Systems, he has taken many courses and been involved in a variety of projects. At his performance review last month Joan gave him a book entitled *Developing Management Proficiency* which he has been reading (with pleasure!). He starts with the list of 50 competencies and first assesses his proficiency with each, followed by his assessment of the importance of each now and over the next 12 months. After reviewing the worksheets, Ben has concluded that he needs to strengthen a few of these competencies – not because he lacks the skills, but because this new assignment will mean he needs to use and apply the competencies in much different ways to be successful. Figure A.1 outlines his focus. The good news, Ben thinks, is that while all these competencies are very important and he needs to develop his proficiency, he is confident that the skill and ability he *does* possess are enough for him to be successful should he decide to accept the assignment. As a result, Ben shifts his thinking slightly, from nervous and fearful to nervous and excited. He knows in his gut that he will probably accept the offer, and turns his focus more on how he will strengthen his competencies and be successful in this assignment.

Questions

Ben plans to research each of the competencies that he's identified. He knows that there is some good content in the study material he used in preparation for his Project Management certification, and he also remembers that there were

Figure A.1 Ben's Competency Needs, Now and in the Future

	Current Time Frame (< 3 mos.)	Future Time Frame (> 3 mos.)
Professional Needs	• Team building • Collaboration • Communication • Goal setting	• Influence • Leadership • Results orientation • Seeking/giving feedback
Personal Needs	• Work-life balance • Stress management	• Work-life balance • Stress management

references provided by the instructor for further reading. He believes that this review will be a necessary foundation but also knows that he needs to talk with others to get more nuanced guidance. Ben has decided that he will need to speak with people inside <u>and</u> outside of NPI. Talking with people in his professional network who he knows lead teams and who have worked on special projects will be very insightful. There are quite a few that he met through the project management study course and several classmates from his undergrad days who are in the area working at other organizations. He also attends regular networking events.

On the other hand, talking with people from inside NPI will be helpful in a different way. Although the questions may be the same or similar, he knows that the responses will be insightful from a different perspective. Every organization has its own culture, Ben thinks, and while NPI is a great place to work he knows that as a new project lead, he will need to build rapport and understand what will work at NPI compared to other organizations. What works in one organization may not be as applicable to another organization. Table A.1 presents the initial questions he wants to ask managers and individual contributors over the next four weeks. Ben will have these questions written down and will be looking for consistency in approach as well as unique ideas from all sources.

Ben makes a list of all the people he wants to reach out to both internally and externally. He's sure he will add to the list, but in the interim, he's glad that he's started keeping track of the ideas about who to interview in his journal.

Observation and Networking

Ben has developed a list of existing cross-functional teams from across the organization (there aren't many), but he wants to investigate this further as he thinks there may be some teams that he's missing. From this list, he's also identified the current team leader. In some cases, it's not clear who the lead is, or it appears there's more than one. He wants to avoid any confusion on the part of others, so he intends to make sure that the project team is identifiable. For his learning strategy, Ben has decided that inviting each one of the team leads to lunch will be helpful to learn. He's come up with the following initial questions:

• What, if any, cultural norms exist across NPI concerning teams and working across boundaries?

- What, if any, barriers exist across the organization?
- What strategy have you used to be successful?
- What support exists in/with upper management?
- Would you mind if I sat in on an upcoming team meeting to observe?
- Are there any resources you would recommend to me?
- What's the one thing you think is the key to your success as a team leader?
- What's the one thing you think I shouldn't do?
- Who else do you recommend I talk to at NPI? Outside of NPI?
- Is there anything else at NPI that you think I should observe or consider?
- What haven't I asked you that I should have asked?

Ben wants to ask these questions face-to-face with others in the organization. He also thinks that doing this one-on-one with some people and in a group setting with others may afford him different perspectives. Ben is even thinking that this strategy may win him supporters, as well. Finally, Ben has written a very short list of senior executives that he thinks will be important to the team's success and his ability to get the team moving quickly in the right direction. He's hoping that Stefan will help facilitate these meetings and perhaps even organize and participate in them. As a side thought, Ben thinks that this in itself will be a significant development opportunity for him. He appreciates Joan and her leadership but has not had as much opportunity to interact and learn from Stefan as he would like. He knows this project is vital to NPI and knows that Stefan, as the executive champion of the project, will be highly invested and engaged.

Role Play

Ben knows that starting the initiative well will be essential. He also knows that some people across the organization will be watching him cautiously. He thinks he is well-liked across NPI but also knows he's untested as a leader. He's participated in "kitchen talk" before when employees informally evaluate leaders and other colleagues – he knows he will be watched and critiqued and that how he sets the tone, both for the team and the organization, will be crucial. His success and the success of the project depend on it. He chatted with Joan about this on Friday, and she offered to help him by role playing some of his opening statements to the team and organization. They also talked about role playing and how he will approach other employees to participate in the team. Stefan will help with this by personally inviting some of the team members, but Ben knows that he has to engage them and keep them motivated and collaborating. Also, some of the team members will be his peers, and this is going to create an interesting dynamic. Some of the role plays he envisions are seen in Table A.2.

In addition to the role plays outlined in Table A.2, Ben likes the idea of doing role plays on his own. He's used this method before without realizing it was a learning tool. The first time he had to do a performance review with his direct report, he was nervous and uncomfortable. To help him prepare, he gave the review to his son's giant stuffed bear a few times until he felt more comfortable with the delivery and the message that he was trying to convey. Ben knows that

Table A.1 Questions for Internal and External Network

Questions for Professional Network	*Questions for People Inside NPI*
• What's the most effective team you've been a part of recently and what made it effective? • What's the most dysfunctional team you've been a part of and what made it dysfunctional? • What are the top 2 or 3 characteristics of a good team leader? • What are some of the mistakes you've seen team leaders make when starting a new team? • What's a good strategy for building a new team quickly? What have you seen work and what have you seen backfire? • What wouldn't you want to see a team leader do or hear him/her say? • What's the one thing you think a leader should do when kicking off a new team? • Do you know anyone I might be able to talk with who was tasked with creating a temporary team for a special project?	• What project teams can you think of at NPI? What's made them successful and what, if anything, has made them struggle? • What's the most effective team you've been a part of at NPI and what made it effective? • What's the most dysfunctional team you've been a part of either here or elsewhere and what made it dysfunctional? • What are the top 2 or 3 characteristics of a good team leader? Why do you say this? • What are some of the mistakes you've seen team leaders make when starting a new team? • What wouldn't you want to see a team leader do or hear him/her say? • What's the one thing you think a leader should do when kicking off a new team? • Is there anyone else inside NPI you think I should speak with? • What's one piece of advice you'd give me?

Table A.2 Role Play Scenarios

Role Plays with Joan	*Role Plays with Other Partners*
• Presentation to upper management pitching the composition of the team • Invitation pitch to team members he plans to invite onto the team • Kick-off meeting • Update meetings with Stefan – who typically wants things completed faster than is realistic • How to solicit feedback from other managers for input into the project	• Conversation with peer who wants to be on the team but who Ben will not invite • Pitch for resources from the marketing team • Discussion with HR about conflicts which may arise when employees have to balance their existing job with the project • Goal-setting conversation • How to solicit feedback from other managers for input into the project

he will need to influence people and that he needs to *be* a leader and be seen as a leader. He's realistic enough to know that he is likely to stumble a time or two in the early part of the project and possibly in the end stages too. Using the role play method to help him prepare for his first review was very helpful, and Ben plans to use this approach to help him on this project journey as well.

Journal

In looking back over the journal he started on Thursday night, Ben is both pleased and a bit unnerved by it. On the one hand, he's managed to capture a considerable amount of information and resources and has charted out much more that he needs to know along with suggestions as to how to get there. On the other hand, it's Sunday night, and he knows Joan and Stefan are expecting an answer in the morning. Ben is confident he can do the job – with a lot of hard work and help from across the organization. He's worried though because the time commitment is enormous and the payoff to his career is not guaranteed. Will his job be available to him once the project is finished? What will be the impact on his family? Will he want to go back to his position in IT? How will he be seen by others in the organization when the project is finished? Ben decides on one final journal exercise before turning in for the night. He lays out the pros and cons of taking the assignment versus turning down the opportunity. He will discuss these with his wife over coffee in the morning, but at the end of the day, Ben knows this will be a gut decision.

Epilogue

After coffee with his wife and talking through the pros and cons of taking the position, Ben's wife agreed that there were good points on both sides of the decision. She also agreed that it was going to be a choice from the gut and that she would support him either way.

When Ben accepted the offer, he told Joan and Stefan that it was with a few caveats – he requested budget money for team building, food (for team meetings and events as well as for engaging others across the organization), and for his own professional development. Joan and Stefan agreed that this was reasonable and said that it was up to Ben to prepare a detailed budget over the next 30 days for the whole project and to pitch this to the Executive Team for approval. Oh wow, thought Ben – here we go!

Index

For Product Safety Concerns and Information please contact our EU
representative GPSR@taylorandfrancis.com
Taylor & Francis Verlag GmbH, Kaufingerstraße 24, 80331 München, Germany